THE ART OF THE WEDDING

RIZZOLI
NEW YORK

New York · Paris · London · Milan

THE ART OF THE WEDDING

INVITATIONS, FLOWERS, DECOR, TABLE SETTINGS, AND CAKES FOR A MEMORABLE CELEBRATION

BY RELAIS & CHATEAUX NORTH AMERICA

INTRODUCTION BY DANIEL HOSTETTLER

TEXT BY JILL SIMPSON

TABLE OF CONTENTS

INTRODUCTION

The collection of hotels, inns, and restaurants of Relais & Châteaux North America are transporting, unique locations that can craft a magical experience for weddings. Each venue offers acclaimed cuisine, personalized service, and unforgettable, authentic architecture and gardens. The location you choose for your wedding will in large part determine the ambience, style, and overall experience of your milestone day. Whether it's an intimate affair tucked away in the mountains of Wyoming, a cosmopolitan dinner in Québec City, or a tented affair on the coast of Rhode Island, the location of a wedding is a genuine expression of a couple.

Within these pages you'll find a collection of real-life couples and their enchanting weddings. Details ranging from invitations, photography, flowers and decor to table settings, menus, ceremonies, receptions, and rehearsal dinners provide inspiration and speak to the identity of each of the Relais & Châteaux properties featured, along with the wisdom of the event coordinators, chefs, and artisans who bring these visions to life.

Relais & Châteaux North America invites you to lose yourself in the enchantment and wonder of Relais & Châteaux weddings, one-of-a-kind places where dreams become reality.

Daniel Hostettler

President, Relais & Châteaux North America

PREVIOUS SPREAD, LEFT: An elated couple says "I do" beneath a floral arbor at The Ranch at Rock Creek. OPPOSITE: Potted topiaries and white rose petals line the aisle leading to a glorious floral ceremony arch at a wedding at Winvian Farm.

A TIMELINE FOR PLANNING YOUR WEDDING

The amount of time needed to plan a wedding can vary greatly, points out Gilda McDaniel, director of weddings at the Fearrington House Inn. If you are open to having a Friday night or Sunday wedding or an off-season date, you won't need to reserve nearly as far ahead as you would for a Saturday night in prime season. But in general, for properties like the Relais & Châteaux venues you'll see in this book, McDaniel offers the following planning timeline as a rule of thumb to help guide your choices:

12–15 MONTHS AHEAD

- Determine your general budget, estimated size of the guest list, and location of your wedding because that will affect every other decision.
- Choose and book your venue. For the most in-demand places and dates, you may need to book even further in advance.
- If you want to work with a wedding planner, get them involved early.
- Reserve or put a hold on hotel rooms.

10–12 MONTHS AHEAD

- Find and book the elements of your wedding that are most important to you—most likely the photographer, band, and florist.
- If you have someone in mind for your officiant, make sure they're available.
- Choose and ask your bridesmaids and groomsmen.

9–10 MONTHS AHEAD

- Shop for your wedding dress.
- Choose a stationer or graphic designer and start working on your save-the-dates, invitations, and other printed materials.
- If you're having a destination wedding or a lot of guests will be traveling to your wedding, send out save-the-dates.
- Plan and book your honeymoon.

8 MONTHS AHEAD

- Register for gifts.
- Decide on the overall look and style of your wedding with your wedding coordinator, planner, or florist.
- Select bridesmaids' dresses.
- Book the rehearsal dinner venue and any other wedding weekend events, such as a welcome cocktail party or farewell brunch.
- Book any additional music needed, such as a string quartet for your ceremony or a DJ for your reception.

6 MONTHS AHEAD

- Meet with the wedding coordinator at your venue to decide on table linens, chairs, menu, and any rentals, such as lounge furniture, a tent, etc. Meet with your florist as well, and conduct any food, cake, and/or wine tastings.
- Choose and order your cake 4–6 months out.
- Book transportation for guests and valet parking, if needed; and a limousine or specialty car for yourselves, if desired.
- Buy or rent the groom's tuxedo or suit and decide on the groomsmen's attire.

3–4 MONTHS AHEAD

- Buy your wedding bands.
- Book a hair and makeup artist.
- Order the invitations and hire a calligrapher, if desired.
- Finalize the menu.
- Select readings, write your vows, if desired, and plan your ceremony with your officiant.
- Decide on favors and/or gift bags if you want them.

2 MONTHS AHEAD

- Send out wedding invitations. Request RSVPs one month before your wedding date.
- Have your wedding gown fitting.
- Get your marriage license.
- Buy gifts for the wedding party.
- Meet with florist to see mock-ups of centerpieces and bouquets.
- Give song suggestions to your band or DJ and ceremony musicians.

3–4 WEEKS AHEAD

- Send the final guest count to your venue.
- Create seating charts; have escort and/or place cards written.
- Have final dress fittings and hair and makeup run-through.

OLD EDWARDS INN & SPA

HIGHLANDS, NORTH CAROLINA

Mountaintop Enchantment

Nestled in the Blue Ridge Mountains, this resort marries a historic inn with modern luxury and an idyllic small-town setting with an expansive farm for hosting country weddings with sophisticated charm.

OPPOSITE: A stunning, free-form bouquet of roses, calla lilies, and wildflowers captures the essence of weddings at Old Edwards Inn & Spa, where weddings are surrounded by and celebrate the beauty of nature.

The mountaintop town of Highlands, North Carolina, is surrounded by breathtaking natural beauty—from stunning waterfalls and verdant forests to dramatic vistas—but it's also known for its vibrant arts community and charming village. In the heart of downtown Highlands, you'll find a picturesque 1878 inn with overflowing flower boxes beckoning from the wrought-iron balconies across its classic brick facade, but Old Edwards is much more than simply an inn. Over time, it has expanded across twelve acres to include a luxurious spa, pools, fitness center, restaurants, and guest cottages. And less than a mile from town is Old Edwards's beautiful thirty-two-acre farm, which was designed specifically to host weddings and events. Inspired by properties in Europe and Napa Valley, the owners completely renovated the original barn, with its lofty, century-old wooden beams and floors and massive stone fireplace, and in 2010 connected it to a soaring, open pavilion to host larger gatherings.

Meander around the idyllic farm setting and you'll discover an enchanting all-white English garden and arbor, a 150-year-old apple and peach orchard, and the original farmhouse, now retrofitted with a salon for wedding-day preparations. Brides can stroll along the lush garden paths for the bridal procession, and outdoor ceremonies or cocktail hours can take place beneath the dappled shade of the orchard. Take note of the welcoming, overstuffed antique furniture and church pews nestled among the apple trees to inspire ideas for enlisting nature's sanctuaries in your own ceremony. Captivating photo opportunities lie around every corner, from a fairy-tale arched bridge over a trout pond to a charming garden folly where the bride can emerge for her walk down the aisle. The buildings are surrounded by lush perennial gardens and a canopy of trees, letting nature paint an exquisite backdrop for the festivities.

OPPOSITE, ABOVE: The facade of the original 1878 brick-front inn is graced with wrought-iron balconies and overflowing window boxes from April until October's first frost. OPPOSITE, BELOW: In the sheltering orchard, 150-year-old trees create a natural cathedral. Here it is set with wooden pews, each capped with an extravagant white floral arrangement. The stunning floral horseshoe at the front is based on a Bermudian wedding tradition. FOLLOWING SPREAD: The orchard was furnished for cocktail hour with overstuffed vintage leather furniture, upholstered settees, and cloth-draped cocktail tables.

OLD
EDWARDS
INN·Spa

The barn and pavilion balance rustic warmth with soaring openness, created by dramatic forty-foot-high ceilings and floor-to-ceiling windows on all sides that slide back completely to create an open-air pavilion. Perusing the wide range of weddings hosted here proves that a barn setting in no way dictates a rustic wedding. The pavilion has been draped in white to look light, airy, and modern; lavished in flowers to create the magic of a springtime arbor; or furnished with antiques for old-world European ambience. Weddings here show how architectural character married with a garden setting establishes a beautiful foundation that's easy to embellish, or can serve as a backdrop to showcase any bride and groom's personal style.

An expansive, open space like the pavilion offers the versatility to set up and furnish it completely differently depending on the style and size of the event. Wedding designers have installed a large, circular bar in the center of the space for an engaging cocktail hour, or set up long, connected tables to make everyone feel as though they're seated all together.

In the South, where large weddings are the norm, people often host "strolling receptions," meaning gourmet stations and passed hors d'oeuvres, rather than sit-down dinners, so that guests can mingle, dance throughout the evening, and eat when and where they choose. The pavilion and outdoor terrace are often set up with a mix of cocktail tables, high-tops, and dining tables to support this flexible approach. Chef Chris Huerta's farm-to-table cuisine showcases the bounty of Old Edwards's five-acre vegetable garden and other local farms, often with a Southern-inflected accent.

The biggest difference that characterizes every Relais & Châteaux property is its unique architectural character and setting, which makes it easy to make each wedding feel one of a kind. As sales manager Melissa Delany notes, "Here, the beautiful grounds and distinctive architecture do all the work for you."

OPPOSITE: For a reception in the pavilion, an all-natural approach to decorating features lush, leafy garlands draped across farmhouse tables, and simple vases displaying green-and-white centerpieces of hydrangeas, ferns, roses, and wildflowers.

MAGNOLIAS AND IVY

The simplicity of this nature-inspired green-and-ivory palette created sophisticated elegance for an early summer wedding. The restraint of the color scheme balanced the lush abundance of the flowers, ferns, and greenery inspired by the forest floor. Creamy white roses, magnolia blossoms with large glossy leaves, feathery astilbes, and leafy boughs were woven through the iron candle chandeliers and spilled out of silver trumpet vases. Tables were draped in a subtly marbleized cloth that evokes wood grain, and lined with floral bouquets large and small nestled in moss and leaves, with clear glass cloches and candleholders that caught the light. Even the classic white cake was adorned with lifelike sugar magnolias and sat atop a bed of magnolia leaves.

OPPOSITE: The bride and groom strolled through the European gardens, showing off her beautifully embroidered, long heirloom lace veil. Stone pathways are lined with abundant greenery and predominantly white flowers, including viburnums, along with touches of pink. A small cottage in the center of the garden can serve as the starting point for the bride and her father or parents to walk to the ceremony.

RIGHT: The pavilion was set for a formal dinner, where everyone was seated together at long tables. A natural palette of green and ivory unified the space, with a dramatic wall of greenery in the background. Roses and greenery were woven into the chandelier, leafed through elegant candelabra, and even wound through the cane chair backs of the bride and groom. They filled tall silver trumpet vases and low mint-julep cups.

GREAT IDEAS FOR CLASSIC ELEGANCE

- A wall covered in greenery at the entrance to the wedding reception area creates a sumptuous botanical backdrop to set off soft whites and ivory.
- Adorn the bride and groom's chairs with roses and vines subtly woven through the cane backs of their seats.
- Long banquet tables for a sit-down dinner create a sense of community where everyone feels joined in celebration.

OPPOSITE: Marbleized tablecloths lent a woodsy accent to the magnolia-and-moss-bedecked tables, along with elegant gilt-edged chargers and rimmed glassware. The napkins were folded to highlight the illustrated menus embellished with wax seals. ABOVE: A grand fireplace is the focal point of the original barn, here set with lounge furniture and the cake table. A classic wedding cake iced in subtle white buttercream "ruffles" was adorned with lifelike sugar magnolias, with magnolia leaves clustered at its base, befitting the natural theme. A magnolia-leaf garland crowned the mantel, flanked on either side by white pillar candles in clear glass hurricanes for modern elegance.

ANIMAL ATTRACTION

Let your personal passions lead the way to a more personalized wedding. This bride's love of alpacas inspired the couple to make them guests of honor at the ceremony and in the wedding photos, and it's hard to imagine anything more adorable. Old Edwards was able to procure this well-trained pair to serve as "attendants," floral wreaths and all, and they—almost—stole the show. If you have a beloved four-legged member of the family such as your dog, or you love horses, think about incorporating them into your wedding for a meaningful touch.

Everything about this wedding celebrated a natural approach. For the rehearsal dinner, a basic wood pergola was constructed outside the barn and lavished with a canopy of cascading vines and classic white roses, creating a sense of shelter and intimacy. An understated table, with a chocolate-brown tablecloth skirting the ground and large, clear glass hurricanes down its center, offered modern simplicity melded with glowing warmth. This romantic setting could be achieved in almost any outdoor space.

For the reception in the pavilion, very simple ivory table runners let the beauty of the wooden farmhouse tables shine through, and lush arrangements of pale peach and yellow flowers added soft color. With the windows fully opened, it felt like eating al fresco.

OPPOSITE: For a bride who adores alpacas, this charming pair joined in the wedding photos wreathed in floral garlands. No doubt they felt right at home in the orchard. FOLLOWING SPREAD: This utterly romantic, rose-covered pergola was erected specially for a rehearsal dinner outside the barn. A simple floor-length tablecloth and a mass of clear glass hurricanes let the leafy floral arbor steal the show.

AUTUMNAL ARTISTRY

People often think of spring and summer for weddings, but in Highlands, North Carolina, as in so many other locales, fall is perhaps the prettiest season of all. The splendor of the mountains in their coat of many colors is breathtaking, and the weather is crisp yet not cold. This bride and groom chose to embrace the season's coziness with an indoor reception by the fire. Carefully orchestrated tables layered pastoral scenes in the china and table runners with a rich mélange of flowers, dried grasses, and seedpods in autumnal hues. Barley-twist candles in colors that match the foliage shimmer from etched-glass hurricanes and pewter candlesticks, while quilted-glass votives refract the golden candlelight, creating an overall effect of inviting warmth and comfort.

The palette was drawn from the bride's exquisite bouquet, a loose and naturalistic composition of a stunning range of flowers, created with an artist's expert eye by weaving together unexpected colors, textures, and varieties. The invitations literally set the scene for the event with a hand-painted watercolor of the mountain setting lining the envelopes and a printed vellum overwrap that mimics pressed flowers. The final grace note was a ruffle-edged cake painted in dreamy watercolor blossoms, with actual blooms emerging from the illustrations for three-dimensional artistry. This wedding is the perfect example of how to carry a simple, seasonal theme through from start to finish, in sophisticated, detailed, and unexpected ways.

OPPOSITE: The bride's naturalistic bouquet was a work of art, weaving in luxuriant heirloom roses, chocolate cosmos, delicate grape hyacinths, sweet peas, and sprigs of berries. It echoed the embroidered lacy flowers on the sheer overlay of a wedding dress that's both modern and elegant.

ABOVE: An autumnal wedding table set before the fire featured woodland patterns, flowers, and foliage. Centerpieces in brass bowls mixed tea-colored roses and white anemones with dried grasses, which were echoed in the leafy fabric runners across each place setting and the pastoral china. Barley-twist candles in pewter candlesticks and cut-glass hurricanes, along with glass votives, brought an inviting glow to the table. OPPOSITE: The floral artistry extended to the cake, with pale flowers painted on its ruffled icing, and real flowers emerging from the painted ones.

FLORAL ABUNDANCE

One approach to successful wedding design is to create a grand gesture. Go all out in one area to set the tone or make a showstopping first impression. For a spring wedding where flowers were the star, guests entered the reception in the pavilion through an enchanting arbor covered in an abundance of roses and hydrangeas in white with touches of pale pink and greenery. Not only did this fashion a dramatic entrance for each guest, but it also perfectly framed a view of the elegant wedding cake.

Inside the pavilion, a three-tiered iron chandelier above a circular bar added for the event provided another opportunity for floral drama, bedecked with a profusion of roses and greenery cascading down from each tier. Creating such an eye-catching focal point at ceiling height is unexpected and allows it to be seen from any point in the room.

Think of every opportunity to weave florals into a location—at Old Edwards Inn, the window boxes along the facade are a well-known feature decorating the balconies, but they're an idea that can be easily adapted to other sites as well.

OPPOSITE, ABOVE: The passageway connecting the pavilion reception space to the original barn was lined for this wedding with an extraordinary arbor adorned with lavish fresh flowers and greenery. The arched arbor framed a view of the wedding cake and connected it to the abundance of flowers cascading across the fireplace mantel. OPPOSITE, BELOW: For this wedding reception, the pavilion was set up with a large, round, custom-built bar, which became both a centerpiece and focal point beneath an iron chandelier bedecked in a stunning array of white and pale pink flowers, lush greenery, and clear crystal orbs. High-top bar tables were placed on either side, and the band and dance floor were situated on the far side of the bar.

THE INN AT DOS BRISAS

WASHINGTON, TEXAS

Boho Luxe

Amid rolling meadows, horse-filled pastures, and fishing ponds in scenic Texas Hill Country, this historic ranch has been transformed into a romantic, pampering resort.

OPPOSITE: Regan and Colin had their first look near the meadow where they got married, accompanied by Monroe, a Belgian Friesian horse with a floral collar as beautiful as Regan's bridal bouquet. The couple chose to take photos before the wedding ceremony, which was timed perfectly to catch "the golden hour."

When Doug Bosch purchased this three-hundred-acre ranch in Texas Hill Country in 2000, it was just meant to be a getaway for his family living in Houston. He was an investor with no background in hospitality. Over time, as they added lodgings for friends and family and a commercial kitchen, he and his wife, Jennifer, started to think about opening a restaurant. "We just got carried away," says Bosch. They opened The Inn at Dos Brisas (Spanish for "two breezes") in 2004, and within just a few years, it was widely praised for its exceptional "pitchfork-to-plate" cuisine and accepted as a member of Relais & Châteaux.

"This is a ranch, but it's not a dude ranch," says Bosch. "It's more polished. Some people ride the horses or fish or hunt, but for the most part people like to sip a glass of wine and watch the 'moving artwork.' There's a sense of elegance and comfort, and endless space where you can truly get away." With just nine Spanish-style haciendas and casitas, the lodgings are quite spacious, extremely private, and appointed in luxury, from the romantic stone fireplaces to the private plunge pools. Each house's patio looks out on tranquil views of the meadows, horses, and ponds.

There are forty-plus acres of certified organic farmland and a seven-thousand-square-foot greenhouse where they grow more than four hundred varieties of organic produce year-round, 80 percent of them heirloom, with more than sixty varieties of tomatoes alone. "Everything is incredibly fresh," says Bosch, "from the field-warm organic tomato that has never seen a refrigerator to the just-laid eggs." Thirteen varieties of lettuce are picked three times daily, for perhaps the freshest salad in Texas. "I don't write down my menu until I'm in the field looking, tasting, and feeling," says Chef Zachary Ladwig, whose menus include meat and poultry, but are centered on the farm's bounty of fresh vegetables.

OPPOSITE: The wedding ceremony took place in a freshly mown meadow, beneath pecan trees draped in Spanish moss. The aisle was lined with Aztec-patterned dhurries and dramatic sprays of pampas grass, chosen to stand out against a verdant backdrop. The stunning ceremony arch was fashioned from pampas grass interwoven with flowers.

When his daughter Regan got engaged and was deciding where to get married, Doug Bosch wooed her with visions of what her wedding on the farm could be like. "I'd always wanted to host a grand wedding and show the place the way it should be shown," says Bosch. "I drove her around to pockets of the property that people often don't see. She ended up getting married in what we now call Regan's Meadow—alongside the creek, hidden from view, and framed by enormous pecan trees covered in Spanish moss."

Regan and Colin's October wedding became an extravagant weekend-long affair in which no expense was spared, but Regan also made sure it had a very welcoming informality. The rehearsal dinner was a Tex-Mex buffet with a margarita bar and long communal tables set up outside the show barn. For the wedding dinner, the Bosches flew in Relais chefs from all over the world, but Regan chose to have food stations rather than a formal seated dinner, and the spacious tent was furnished with linen-upholstered lounge furniture, in addition to dining tables, so people could mingle, dine, and dance as they felt like it.

While the style of the rehearsal dinner was richly colored, with exuberant flowers in a Frida Kahlo palette, the wedding and reception featured a more subdued natural palette and boho luxe vibe. The wedding aisle was lined with dramatic pampas grass arrangements flanking pale Aztec-motif rugs, with a stunning pampas grass and floral arch at the front. That color scheme carried over into the reception with romantic dried-flower chandeliers hung from the tent ceiling and handwoven dream catchers adorning the bar.

Though the mood was relaxed, every last detail was thought through, from the elaborate gift bags to an artisan hand-rolling cigars for guests at the reception. In the end, Doug, Regan, and the staff created the wedding of everyone's dreams.

OPPOSITE: Inside a spacious sailcloth tent, floral chandeliers, airy diamond structures, and pampas grass halos hung from the ceiling. Only the family and wedding party had arranged seating; all the other tables and lounge areas were designed for people to eat, dance, and mingle throughout the evening. Food stations served everything from a raw bar to heritage pork loin and salt-baked wahoo to farm-fresh ratatouille.

ABOVE, FROM LEFT: During their recessional, Regan and Colin had guests throw lavender seeds, in hopes that it would seed a path of wildflowers in the spot where they married. Boutonnieres were a mix of roses, scabiosas, and other blooms. Signature cocktails were garnished with fresh sprigs of lavender. Embroidered white tablecloths were adorned with pale pink and white flower arrangements interspersed with lanterns and candles.

GREAT IDEAS FOR BOHO CHARM

- For an outdoor wedding, delineate the aisle with flat-woven rugs and pampas grass arrangements. The light, neutral hue of pampas grass stands out well against a backdrop of trees and grass.
- Time transitions carefully. This couple had their cocktail hour and photos before the ceremony, so that afterward guests could go straight to dinner and the reception.
- Have a cigar roller making custom cigars for guests as a special, unexpected amenity.
- Set up a photo booth in a vintage VW van, like Regan and Colin did, for a fun twist.
- Hire plenty of waitstaff so that guests don't have to line up at the bar but can have cocktails and drink refills brought to them directly.
- If your ceremony is in a field or lawn, have guests throw flower seeds instead of birdseed and seed a wildflower meadow.

ABOVE: Instead of one large wedding cake, a trio of boho-glam multilayered cakes expanded the decorative possibilities. The cakes mixed lustrous gilding, painted pastel florals and feathers, a monogram, and modern geo patterns, for a dazzling dessert buffet. OPPOSITE: French furniture upholstered in natural linen, with four-sided tufted banquettes crowned with dramatic floral arrangements, vintage tables, Moroccan wedding blankets, and pastel silk pillows created an elegant lounge area in the spacious tent. Custom whitewashed floors kept the look light and airy. In lieu of a sit-down dinner, everyone could dine, lounge, and dance throughout the evening.

ABOVE, OPPOSITE, AND FOLLOWING SPREAD: The rehearsal dinner was held in a field outside the ranch's show barn and equestrian arena (the backup location in case of inclement weather). Exuberant arrangements of bright pink and orange garden roses and other flowers on colorful patterned tablecloths set a festive feel for a Tex-Mex dinner. A buffet with farm-fresh organic salsa and guacamole, taco and fajita fixings, a margarita bar, and long communal tables created an invitingly informal, interactive meal where everyone could get to know each other. String lights and candles added a romantic glow as the sun set.

Invitations

Invitations and printed accessories are very much a part of the trend toward personalization and customization in weddings. "I approach designing the wedding suite from a branding perspective," notes Emily Hostetler, owner of Paper Moss in Boston, and designer of the invitation suite seen on page 118. Here, her pointers on paper goods:

- Start by gathering anything that inspires you. It can be a gift tag, your wedding dress, a textile you love. Anything that makes your heart leap a little.
- Have your stationer design the whole suite, from save-the-dates to programs, so they all work together. Hostetler has even designed custom lobster bibs, coasters, confetti, and ties for the groomsmen with a custom monogram.
- Don't use the same monogram or motif in the same way on everything. "We design interrelated graphic elements, and then weave variations throughout the whole suite," says Hostetler.
- Make it personal. One couple's nicknames for each other were "llama" and "lobster," and Hostetler included those motifs in their monogram.
- Illustrations add a special touch. If the reception is taking place in a historic building, consider having a watercolor illustration or pen-and-ink sketch made of it for your invitation. Or create a hand-drawn map of the area or use illustrations to represent each activity on the schedule.
- It's worth having addresses hand-calligraphed on the envelopes if you can, because that's everyone's first impression.

RIGHT AND OPPOSITE: Custom-painted watercolor illustrations, ornate die-cut or printed vellum "belly bands" that wrap around the invitation suite, letterpress printing, and handmade papers are just some of the ways to add a unique touch to your invitations. Your stationer can design everything from the program to the seals for your goodie bags.

THE TWELFTH OF OCTOBER

TAKE A HIKE

J&C

Regan Colin
OCTOBER 15, 2016
THE INN AT DOS BRISAS
Ceremony
PROCESSIONAL
BRIDAL ENTRANCE
WELCOME ADDRESS TO FAMILY + FRIENDS
FAMILY BLESSING
COMMUNITY VOWS
EXCHANGE OF VOWS

THE FEARRINGTON HOUSE INN

PITTSBORO, NORTH CAROLINA

Rural Reverie

Scenic pastures of Piedmont farmland surround a picturesque village inspired by the hamlets of England, with a world-class restaurant, inn, gardens, and barn, for rural weddings with a touch of elegance.

OPPOSITE: A couple posed for a post-wedding kiss in front of the Fearrington barn. Receptions are usually held in the 1927 barn, whose original exterior has been preserved. A vine-covered pergola at the entrance and twinkling branches and grapevine balls welcome guests inside.

In 1974, a young couple named R. B. and Jenny Fitch bought a 640-acre farm and farmhouse with an eye to creating a "coming-together place" like the tiny villages they had fallen in love with visiting England. They converted the columned farmhouse into a fine restaurant and Jenny, a true renaissance woman, served as the first executive chef and also designed the interiors, created the gardens, and arranged the flowers. Rather than tearing down or modernizing, the Fitches aimed to preserve the bucolic farmland and simple white farm buildings as much as possible. They began developing a village center by repurposing the existing structures: the granary became a market and deli, the milking barn soon housed a shop, and the old barn became the site of a farmers' market and eventually, home to weddings and events.

If Fearrington has a warm, homey feeling, perhaps that's because it started as a home, and that's where the restaurant is still housed today, even as the village has grown around it to encompass a spa, boutiques, café, beer garden, and an inn with thirty-two beautifully appointed rooms. The barn has retained its original 1927 character, but was updated to include a kitchen, climate control system, and other amenities. The property still incorporates a working farm, where distinctive Belted Galloway cows can be seen grazing in the pastures, and vegetable and herb gardens supply food for the restaurant.

RIGHT: Jenny's Garden, named for Jenny Fitch, who planted the first gardens at Fearrington, features a beautiful garden terrace framed by pergolas and arbors around a central fountain. Small weddings (under fifty people) can be held here, and it's a favorite spot for photos of the wedding party.

Fearrington is a storybook location for weddings thanks to its pastoral setting, elegant gardens, spacious barn, exquisite cuisine, and top-notch personal service, helmed by longtime wedding planner Gilda McDaniel. Fearrington is unusual in that almost everything can be created on-site, from the floral arrangements and decor to the wedding cake, which allows for a streamlined, less stressful experience.

The executive chef, Colin Bedford, hails from England, but he draws on the bounty of the Fearrington gardens and other local farms to craft menus that meld the best of traditional Southern cuisine with his European training.

Though the barn is nearly a century old, the rustic grandeur of its soaring, double-height space and the graceful simplicity of its latticed wood rafters, adorned with natural twig chandeliers, melds down-home style with haute touches. It has welcoming character but also a chameleon-like ability to transform from classic farmhouse to elegant garden to modern loft, depending on the furnishings and decor. Ceremonies can be held outside at one of several beautiful gardens on the property, and smaller celebrations can be hosted in the garden terrace.

Weddings here offer inspiration for seamlessly choreographing outdoor and indoor elements and adding sophisticated, polished beauty to an inviting rustic setting—the true definition of Southern hospitality.

OPPOSITE: The classic 1927 farmhouse is now the Fearrington House Restaurant. In 1986, the owners built the Fearrington House Inn, adding luxurious accommodations in order to be eligible for Relais & Châteaux membership.

IN BLOOM

So much of the joy of a wedding is in the anticipation—for the bride and groom, but also for their families and guests. An enticing invitation that captures the spirit and style of the event is the first step in setting the tone and whetting everyone's excitement for the special day. For the picture-perfect June wedding of a young couple who met at a nearby university, a charming watercolor painting of the Fearrington barn on the wedding invitation let out-of-town guests get a feeling for the venue from the first glance. The same artistry was carried through to the painted floral monogram crest on the welcome signs, menus, and place cards.

The design team created a captivating first impression and gave the weathered barn's simple entrance a sense of presence by adding a pergola with cascading Lady Banks' roses and camellias, and softly draped curtains framing the opening. In the garden and terrace as well as inside the barn, upholstered lounge furniture in neutrals and soft pastels and skirted tables brought a level of sophistication to the natural setting. Fulsome bouquets of peonies and garden roses, from the Fearrington gardens and elsewhere, became a stunning focal point, elevated in tall, clear glass vases on the front tables and cascading down the longer banquet tables and across the stage for the musicians. Elegant crystal chandeliers elevated the barn's rustic twig ones, and string lights twinkled across the rafters. White fabric draped from the ceiling, a gleaming white dance floor, white tablecloths, and a shimmering curtained backdrop for the band all helped lighten the rough-hewn interior. From the bridal bouquet and boutonnieres to the centerpieces and the cake, the full-bloom roses and peonies in pale pink, white, and cream paired with abundant greenery captured the naturalistic feel of a garden, connecting indoors to out, and the eternal sunshine of a beautiful June day.

OPPOSITE: This bride and groom posed by the fence line, with Fearrington's distinctive Belted Galloway cows in the background.

Mr. and Mrs. Wade Kordell Jones
request the honor of your presence
at the marriage of their daughter
Harper Rae
to
Tyson Hardy Creech II
son of Mr. and Mrs. W. Hardy Creech II
Saturday, the fifteenth of June
two thousand nineteen
at five o'clock in the evening
University Presbyterian Church
Chapel Hill, North Carolina

LEFT: A charming watercolor illustration of the Fearrington barn on the invitation gave guests a peek at the wedding venue and its amiable country style. PAGES 60 AND 61: Fearrington's in-house florists created the bouquets and boutonnieres using a mix of flowers from their gardens as well as other growers. White roses and greens created handsome boutonnieres, while full-blown peonies and garden roses in whisper-pale pastels made up the bride's bouquet.

ABOVE, FROM LEFT: The garden terrace was set with lounge furniture and even rugs for the cocktail hour. Signs featuring a custom floral crest designed for the new couple directed guests where to go. FOLLOWING SPREAD: The barn's interior was filled with lavish bouquets of white and pink peonies and roses on each table and across the stage. White fabric draped across the ceiling, and crystal chandeliers in addition to the regular twig ones brightened the lofty interior.

GREAT IDEAS FOR BARN WEDDINGS

- Commission an illustration of your wedding venue or a custom crest with your initials, which you can use on everything from invitations to signs, escort cards, napkins, and gift bags.
- A barn can make for a rustic, relaxed reception space or, through lighting, furniture, and flowers, can be transformed into a more elegant venue.
- Rent some comfortable lounge furniture for the cocktail hour to create seating groups and set a sophisticated style for the event.
- Pastel flowers are always beautiful, but consider brighter hues or darker accents to stand out against the wood.
- If you want to accommodate more guests than your venue can usually seat, consider placing buffet serving tables or the dance floor in an adjacent tented space. Or do buffet stations with more informal seating instead of a sit-down dinner.

NATURAL BEAUTY

The bride grew up in nearby Durham, North Carolina, but she had moved to Manhattan to work for a big tech firm. For her wedding, she returned to her hometown roots, and showed her city friends the welcoming warmth of Southern hospitality. Fearrington offers five different garden spots in which to host a ceremony, and the largest, Willow Oaks, with its graceful latticed arbor entwined with ivy, was an ideal setting on this sparkling spring day. The bride's natural radiance shines through in every photograph. The classic elegance of her dress was complemented by a garden-fresh bouquet of white, pink, and mauve blossoms, while her bridesmaids' bouquets were all-white wildflowers, like those marking each row of seats at the ceremony. The reception in the barn similarly celebrated country simplicity, with wildflowers in humble mason jars, vintage clipboard table numbers, and classic wooden farmhouse tables peeking through lacy runners. As the sun set on the joyous celebration, grapevine balls lit with fairy lights twinkled from the trees.

OPPOSITE: The huge, joyful smiles of the just married. This couple's ceremony took place under the elegant arbor in the Willow Oaks garden.

ABOVE AND OPPOSITE: Each bridesmaid chose her own dress in a mix of jewel tones, complemented by all-white bouquets. The groomsmen shared a post-wedding toast. FOLLOWING SPREAD: Simple farmhouse tables showed off ivory lace runners, with crimson and white bouquets in mason jars and clipboard table numbers for a vintage country feel in the barn.

3
CHAMPAIGN

TROPICAL PUNCH

Refreshingly bold and less expected, the bright colors and dramatic forms of tropically inspired flowers set a vibrant tone for this autumn morning wedding. The Fearrington's own floral designers did the bouquets and arrangements, marrying brilliant red, deep coral, and 'Polynesian Punch' roses with orange and purple calla lilies and freesia to lend a lush tropical feel that popped against the brides' ethereal white wedding dresses. The wedding took place outdoors beneath the arbor in Jenny's Garden, named for the founder of Fearrington House, who created the gardens. The reception was held in the Garden Terrace, a white and airy pavilion on the Fearrington grounds. The same enticing floral palette carried through to centerpieces spilling out of rustic lanterns and the wedding cake.

The brides chose similar, but different lacy white wedding gowns, and had their beloved dogs as escorts. Each bride had her father walk her down the aisle. Also less expected was their choice of a morning wedding and reception because breakfast is their favorite meal of the day. It pays to center your wedding on your own preferences and loves, because that will not only make it distinctive, but also the most personal and meaningful to you.

OPPOSITE: Beautiful symmetry: the two brides, in similarly lacy gowns, were flanked by a pair of lush floral arrangements with hydrangeas sparked with bright orange roses, beneath a garden pergola framed in ivy.

ABOVE AND OPPOSITE, TOP RIGHT: The brides are standing in front of the Fearrington House Restaurant. OPPOSITE: ABOVE LEFT AND BELOW: The vibrant, fresh floral palette of coral, red, and purple in roses, calla lilies, and berries extended from the bridal bouquets to the centerpieces nestled in wooden lanterns to the cake.

WEEKAPAUG INN

WESTERLY, RHODE ISLAND

Coastal Serenity

With classic Shingle-style architecture on a beautiful saltwater pond, Weekapaug Inn prizes nature, simplicity, and the laid-back, intimate charms of its New England coastal setting.

OPPOSITE: This couple's beloved goldendoodle played a part in their wedding as "flower dog," and joined them on the beach near Weekapaug for a photo before the ceremony.

PRIORITY

Nestled on the Rhode Island shoreline overlooking Quonochontaug Pond and the Atlantic Ocean just beyond it, Weekapaug Inn is a hidden gem a bit more off the beaten path than its Watch Hill neighbors and its sister inn, Ocean House. The natural beauty of the dunes and grasses on this protected estuary are reflected in the weathered cedar shingles and low-profile, rambling architecture of this storied inn with just thirty-one rooms and suites. The original Weekapaug Inn was built in 1899 but had to be completely rebuilt in 1939 after it was damaged in a hurricane. The owners wisely chose to relocate it off the ocean, facing the pond, to protect the barrier beach and dunes. In 2012, it was completely renovated to preserve the best of the past while retrofitting it with modern amenities. The inn is listed in the National Register of Historic Places, but its quiet luxuries are thoroughly up-to-date. Each room boasts its own unique scenic view, layout, and furnishings.

Weekapaug is designed to encourage guests to unplug and reconnect with nature: The rooms have no TVs or phones, except by request, and the windows open to welcome in salt-air breezes and the soothing lull of the ocean. There is a plethora of waterfront activities, a staff naturalist leads nature walks and bird-watching, and the lawn is home to old-fashioned pastimes like shuffleboard and bocce.

Weddings here tend to be more relaxed and focused on the outdoors and natural environs. While small weddings and ceremonies can take place indoors all year-round, most couples choose to host their ceremony overlooking the golden pond, and their reception beneath the open-air sailcloth tent. "The Weekapaug is understated, barefoot elegance, like you're entertaining in a garden by the sea, beside tall grasses bordering the pond," says Lauren DiStefano, special events manager. "Receptions are often a little more rustic, in keeping with the backdrop." Taking cues for your decor and palette from the surroundings is an easy, natural way to create a seamless look and experience for any outdoor wedding.

The chef's modern interpretation of New England coastal cuisine features fresh-off-the-boat seafood, produce from local farms, and native foraging.

In fashioning a wedding that's as natural as the ebb and flow of the tides, both couples and guests are placed at ease to truly enjoy the weekend's events in a spectacular setting.

OPPOSITE: The classic New England Shingle-style exterior of the 1939 inn fits in naturally with the beach grasses and fieldstone walls. The inn looks out onto Quonochontaug Pond and also offers a saltwater swimming pool. Bicycles are always on hand for scenic rides—as are kayaks, paddleboards, sailboats, and fishing rods, for plenty of activities to keep the wedding party and guests active together.

THE NATURALS

For their September wedding, this couple took inspiration from the weathered, seaside palette of sand dunes and beach grasses, wildflowers and driftwood, and the picturesque stone walls and crushed-shell paths around the Weekapaug Inn. Instead of more predictable pink roses or blue hydrangeas, they opted for all-natural but quite dramatic decor using grandly scaled pampas grass centerpieces paired with more than thirty airy woven-rattan pendants of various shapes and sizes. Weathered wood bistro chairs and taupe napkins echoed the neutral palette, while smaller bouquets on the tables of blush and creamy white dahlias, dramatic protea, feathery pink astilbes, and silvery eucalyptus branches added beachy whispers of color. Taking your color cues from the natural environs, particularly for an outdoor wedding, is a no-fail approach that creates a setting totally in tune with the environment wherever you are.

Though rain ushered their ceremony indoors to the inn's Sea Room, that only made it feel more intimate and cozy, says the bride. The outdoor reception, held beneath an airy white tent, continued as planned, and personal touches abounded that infused it with meaning: The couple's beloved goldendoodle served as "flower dog," sporting a charming leafy garland. Names were calligraphed onto pieces of sea glass for escort cards, in a perfect nod to the setting. But the most personal element was the gray-and-white ticking stripe aprons the groom's mother hand-sewed for each guest, embroidered with the geographic coordinates of the location, so that everyone could fully enjoy the lobster dinner without worry—a thoughtful and imaginative keepsake that guests will enjoy and actually use for years.

OPPOSITE: For a bride who didn't want the expected roses, stunning blush dahlias, wispy astilbes, sea oats, silver-dollar eucalyptuses, and even sprigs of rosemary created a bouquet filled with texture and fragrance.

RIGHT: The reception's distinctive natural decor mixed dramatic pampas grass arrangements in tall glass vases and hanging from the tent ceiling, along with an eclectic mix of airy, woven lanterns. Bleached wood bistro chairs and simple ivory tablecloths and taupe napkins complemented the driftwood palette.

GREAT IDEAS FOR COASTAL WEDDINGS

- Hang rattan lanterns from the ceiling of a tent or room for a beachy, modern alternative to chandeliers.
- Tall centerpieces of grasses or branches are more dramatic than flowers and create a neutral, earthy palette.
- Give your beloved dog a collar of greenery or flowers and include them in the wedding or photos.
- Cloth aprons or lobster bibs make a thoughtful and practical favor for a seafood dinner.
- Hand-calligraph names onto sea glass or shells for escort cards.

ABOVE, LEFT: The invitation suite previewed the sense of subdued, elegant simplicity that would be showcased in the wedding. Modern initials were highlighted in gold foil against a sophisticated gray-green background. ABOVE, RIGHT: In addition to the tall arrangements of grasses, smaller bouquets of proteas, dahlias, blue thistles, and blush astilbes lent a beachy elegance to the tables. OPPOSITE: The bride and groom shared an intimate moment at the head table. The groom's mother hand-sewed ticking-stripe aprons for every guest to wear to protect their clothes while eating lobster at the reception. The aprons were embroidered with the longitude and latitude of the wedding location for a memorable (and useful) favor.

THE RANCH AT ROCK CREEK

PHILIPSBURG, MONTANA

Romantic Frontier

Beneath the endless sky, rocky peaks, and fly-fishing streams of western Montana, enjoy ranch life in the great outdoors with a luxurious twist.

OPPOSITE: For a winter wedding on a carpet of snow, this intrepid couple said their "I do's" in front of a beautiful tree-limb altar garlanded in festive red flowers and berries, dried hydrangeas, pinecones, and evergreens for a holiday feel. Red rose petals dusted the snow.

Tucked within a particularly picturesque, unspoiled Montana valley, with a Blue Ribbon trout stream running through it and the Pintler Mountains as a majestic backdrop, The Ranch at Rock Creek unfolds across 6,600 acres of pristine prairie. It is centered on the original nineteenth-century homestead and barn, which have been restored as authentic, yet luxurious, frontier accommodations, joined by a lodge, log cabins, streamside glamping tents, and even Conestoga covered wagons for would-be pioneers. The ranch is home to a herd of seventy horses and 150 head of cattle. This all-inclusive, exclusive resort can host up to 125 people and offers a broad range of outdoor activities to enjoy in its breathtaking setting.

"What people love about having weddings here is that it's not just about the ceremony," says Jon Martin, general manager of The Ranch at Rock Creek. "It's a whole weekend-long experience. The only people on the property are those attending the wedding, and everyone can go off and have different amazing adventures during the day and then come back and share them with one another over dinner. Whether it's a trail ride, hiking to the 'Top of the World,' or fly-fishing on a Blue Ribbon stream, it's a much bigger experience than a five-hour wedding."

Weddings are typically a three-day affair in the late spring, early summer, or winter and might incorporate anything from a rodeo to a barn dance and pig roast to a whiskey tasting in the tack room or a late-night bonfire beneath star-strewn skies. Delicious ranch-inspired gourmet meals from Chef Josh Drage might be cooked outdoors on a wood-fired grill, on a campfire Dutch oven, or in a state-of-the-art kitchen and include Wagyu beef, wild game, and locally grown organic produce.

Brides and grooms typically want to have their ceremony outdoors in the awe-inspiring surroundings, but in case of inclement weather, there's also the spacious Buckle Barn, which was constructed with reclaimed wood from an old ranch nearby. "There are seven or eight

PREVIOUS SPREAD: After getting ready in Bluebird Cabin, in the background, a bride and her bridesmaids, all in white, walked across a meadow to River House, the original nineteenth-century homestead. The wedding ceremony was held there on the lawn overlooking Rock Creek. OPPOSITE, ABOVE: A hand-forged sign marks the entrance to The Ranch at Rock Creek. Weddings are generally held in the late spring, early summer, and winter, when the ranch has more availability. OPPOSITE, BELOW: Bluebird Cabin has a screened-in porch that sits right on the creek. Even newer cabins like this one were built to fit in seamlessly with the nineteenth-century originals.

THE RANCH AT ROCK CREEK
RC

different locations where we've had ceremonies, including atop Paradise Mountain," says Martin. "One of the best things I've seen is where we've timed the running of the horses with the pronouncement, 'You may now kiss the bride.' It was a beautiful mountaintop ceremony, and in the valley below was our herd of seventy horses just thundering across the pasture as the couple kissed."

At the end of their wedding celebration, many newlywed couples like to escape to Trapper Cabin, which is a mile upstream, away from everything, with a firepit outside and a soaking tub on the deck, for the ultimate romantic hideaway.

"People take pride in the experience of their wedding and what the memories of it are," Martin notes. "No matter how great the flowers or the meal in a more conventional setting, people will feel like they've been to something similar, whereas here, there is truly nothing else like it."

OPPOSITE: The bride and groom shared a special toast on the mountaintop dubbed "Top of the World," at a table set with cowhide chairs. It's hard to imagine a more magnificent setting in which to celebrate, just the two of you. ABOVE: At the reception, centerpieces matched the bridal bouquet, with white flowers and greenery "planted" naturally in a stoneware bowl.

RIGHT: For a small wedding, hand calligraphy gave the invitations a very personal feel and timeless artistry. The white lettering on slate-blue, deckle-edge paper was refreshingly different while still feeling classic. The same calligrapher addressed the envelopes and painted guests' names on river rocks to serve as place cards, perfectly fitting for the site. Many photographers can create a vignette like this of the invitation suite, including the engagement ring in a vintage ring box, for a beautifully composed picture.

WATCHMAKERS & JEWELLERS
Dunstall & Co.
10 KING ST.
GRAVESEND
Celia Avery
&
Gerard Lincoln
request the pleasure of
your company at their
marriage celebration
Saturday, September 10th
SHAKESPEARE
Mr and Mrs Collin Pierce
1742 Greenview Street
Ashland, Montana
5 9 0 0 3

ABOVE AND OPPOSITE: For an early September wedding, the bride carried a naturalistic bouquet that interspersed peonies and hydrangeas with grasses, wildflowers, herbs, and berries, in a pared-back green-and-white palette.

RIGHT: Although the barn is rustic, it can host elegant receptions with equal aplomb. Sophisticated gray tablecloths made lush centerpieces with pink and white roses pop, and complemented the silver-rimmed glass chargers and a mix of vintage silverware. Printed menus with a sprig of olive leaves were a natural touch. Round tables are always a nice choice for encouraging conversation among everyone.

ON TOP OF THE WORLD

One treasured spot for couples to marry at The Ranch at Rock Creek is atop Paradise Peak. Also a favorite hike, it's perfect for weddings, as ranch vehicles transport guests up to the peak, then park out of view until after the ceremony. For this June wedding, a wooden platform and benches were set up overlooking the spectacular view of the valley, with the view framed by gorgeous floral pillars of roses in pale, sun-washed hues and greenery. Similar arrangements were placed at the end of each pew. As the ceremony ended, guests were treated to the awe-inspiring sight of the herd of seventy horses thundering across the valley. A vintage truck from the ranch picked up the newlyweds to take them to the dinner in the Buckle Barn, which was dressed simply in greenery and lights twined around its pillars, and long wooden farm tables lined with bouquets of lush peach peonies. A spectacular, yet very natural-looking, cake was adorned with woodland flowers woven into grapevines encircling its four layers. After dinner, dancing took place in a clear tent lined in fairy lights, echoing the nighttime Montana sky, filled with a million stars.

OPPOSITE: The couple enjoyed a moment of togetherness after their wedding ceremony, walking through the meadows on "Top of the World."

RIGHT: The ceremony was held atop Paradise Peak, where the natural majesty matched the meaningfulness of the ceremony. An asymmetric altar framed the view with pillars of roses and greenery, which were echoed in the arrangements at the foot of each pew. At The Ranch at Rock Creek, there are no set locations where the ceremony has to take place—you are free to choose almost any spot.

ABOVE: A vintage truck from the ranch served as a fitting getaway vehicle for the bride and groom. OPPOSITE: The wedding dinner brought everyone together at long, family-style tables inside the Buckle Barn. Rustic elegance prevailed, with simple farmhouse tables, industrial-style metal chairs, and a row of centerpieces that mixed peach peonies with the varied textures of wildflowers, thistles, berries, roses, and purply leaves.

ABOVE, LEFT AND RIGHT: The floral palette fit the worn wood and natural materials of the ranch, with pale, dusty roses and sprigs of wildflowers creating a flower bed to hold table numbers slipped onto twigs. The same flowers were clustered in simple glass vases. OPPOSITE: The charming wedding cake, on a rustic wooden pedestal, proves that less is more: a bramble of vines wreathes its four layers, with small flowers, seedpods, and leaves artfully woven in.

ABOVE: After the dinner, dancing took place outside in a clear tent lined with strings of fairy lights, for dancing under the stars. OPPOSITE: At the combined welcome and rehearsal dinner the previous evening, everyone enjoyed a hearty outdoor chuckwagon supper and a big bonfire, sitting on blanket-draped hay bales, as friends and family toasted the couple.

GREAT IDEAS FOR MOUNTAIN WEDDINGS

- Consider holding your ceremony in a favorite scenic spot, whether it's a mountaintop, meadow, or beach (with a backup plan for inclement weather, of course, and a way to transport guests to the site).
- Take a bit of time after the ceremony to escape, just the two of you, to savor the moment before you join your guests for cocktails.
- A casual outdoor cookout for a rehearsal or welcome dinner can be a great icebreaker for the two families and groups of friends to get to know one another, and a bonfire draws everyone together.
- A clear tent can make you feel even more a part of the outdoors in a beautiful location.
- If your family and close friends are able to travel, a destination wedding weekend in an intimate setting can create indelible memories for you and your guests.

Flowers

"Flowers have become exponentially more important over the past five years," says Yumiko Fletcher, owner of Hana Floral Design in Mystic, Connecticut, and the florist behind the weddings shown at Ocean House and Weekapaug Inn. "Many couples want to create a 'Wow!' moment, whether that's a spectacular floral arch for the ceremony or an eye-catching floral installation over the dance floor."

"Flower arrangements are more organic in feel, and more garden-inspired," notes Bett Foley, principal floral designer at the Fearrington House Inn. "People are using more foliage and vines, as well as grasses and dried flowers." Bridal bouquets are also often more organic and asymmetrical in form. Some advice from Foley and Fletcher:

- In addition to gathering photos you like from Instagram or Pinterest, and pictures of your dresses and color palette, give your florist a few adjectives that describe the feeling you want for the day—modern, romantic, natural, and so on.
- The bridal bouquet is the most personal and most photographed element, so make it a focal point.
- Make your decor personal. Foley had one couple of Indian heritage who incorporated small elephant figurines as candleholders and bud vases. For another bride who was an author and book lover, Foley incorporated stacks of books into the table arrangements.
- At a large wedding, it's nice to vary the centerpieces so they look less cookie-cutter, but keep them connected. Maybe some tables have more foliage and lanterns, or some tables have tall arrangements and others low.
- Aisle planters and arrangements used for the ceremony can be moved to the reception and repurposed in front of the stage or another area.

RIGHT AND OPPOSITE: Let your flowers express the season, from spring peonies and summer roses to autumn hydrangeas and dahlias.

Christian Louboutin

OCEAN HOUSE

WATCH HILL, RHODE ISLAND

Seaside Romance

Perched overlooking the sea in the historic summer community of Watch Hill, Ocean House transports Gilded Age hospitality into the modern day, offering the oceanfront wedding of your dreams.

OPPOSITE: For a bride who'd grown up spending summers in Rhode Island, a seaside wedding invited guests to share in her childhood memories and love of the ocean. Her floral-embroidered gown perfectly echoed an abundant bouquet of peonies, garden roses, and summer blooms.

For many couples, getting married by the water is a longtime fantasy. Whether it's inspired by childhood vacation memories, the romance of the sea, or the invitingly relaxed feel of a beach house, the seaside calls its siren song. Ocean House, in Watch Hill, Rhode Island, has been enticing couples and families for over a century to this storied oceanfront hotel, where old-fashioned elegance meets the barefoot, salt-tinged ease of the beach. Like its more extravagant coastal cousin, Newport, Watch Hill developed as a summer getaway for wealthy city families at the turn of the last century. They built grand Victorian "cottages" along the coast, many of which were unfortunately destroyed by hurricanes or fires over the course of the twentieth century. Ocean House, originally built in 1868, soon after the Civil War, survived, but over many decades, it sadly fell into neglect and disrepair. It was sold in 2004 and then painstakingly rebuilt by devoted new owners. The landmark yellow exterior was replicated almost exactly, with all 247 windows in the same places, but the interior was reconfigured to provide more spacious, luxurious accommodations, with forty-nine rooms and eighteen suites. Ocean House blends the best of old and new, with a spa, five-star restaurant, gardens, a curated art collection, and library wine cellar commingling with old-fashioned pastimes like croquet, shuffleboard, and rocking chair porches. The resort encompasses thirteen waterfront acres and a private white-sand beach.

While the hotel has a beautiful seaside ballroom that can hold 160 guests, Ocean House is best known for its glamorous tented receptions on the lawn or beach. The wedding staff at Ocean House has an exclusive partnership with a talented team of designers to truly customize every aspect of the decor for each couple, for an especially creative, personal feel. "Aesthetically, Ocean House offers refined glamour with those 'wow' moments," says Lauren DiStefano, special events manager. "You feel transported to an earlier era of elegance." The outdoor seaside setting is always magical, but the design team strives to make the atmosphere beneath the tent poles equally captivating.

OPPOSITE: When the Ocean House was rebuilt in 2004, its beloved yellow exterior remained almost exactly the same, but its interiors were completely reconfigured and updated. The hotel faces onto the Atlantic Ocean, with dune grasses and wild roses carpeting the grounds leading down to the private beach. FOLLOWING SPREAD: Guests walked from the ceremony at the Watch Hill Chapel, which dates from 1875, to the seaside reception at the Ocean House.

OCEAN HOUSE

The cuisine at Ocean House, which changes daily, not just seasonally, is naturally focused on New England seafood and the freshest ingredients from local farms, with hints of French and Italian influences. But weddings can feature anything from a lobster boil to barbecue, depending on the couple's taste.

For many couples who choose to wed at Ocean House, weddings become a weekend-long affair, featuring not only the ceremony and reception, but also welcome cocktails on the beach, a rehearsal dinner, morning yoga or golf, ocean swims and beach walks, and a delicious farewell brunch.

In the end, even for guests who've only traveled within the state, weddings here feel like a wonderful vacation getaway that's a world away from everyday life.

OPPOSITE: The custom-designed invitation suite featured a liner and motifs that echoed the intricate embroidered flowers on the bride's gown, designed by Carolina Herrera. ABOVE: The bride and groom got ready for the wedding; the bride, at her parents' nearby summer house.

FLIGHT OF FANCY

For a young couple who met by chance on a delayed flight home from New Orleans, the theme of flight was subtly woven into their wedding through the poetic motif of butterflies, which flitted across the beribboned tent and across place cards and centerpieces, even alighting on the wedding cake. The butterflies' colorful ebullience was reflected in the kaleidoscope of streamers draped across the tent ceiling and the vibrant centerpieces spilling out of charming birdcages, instantly setting a mood of cheerful exuberance and whimsy. This creative, captivating theme proves how a little imagination can completely transform a standard white tent. The lush, almost overgrown floral arrangements featured dramatically tall branches and vines in some places, and full-blown coral and pink roses, orange ranunculuses, lavender sweet peas, peonies, and hydrangeas weaving their way through the gilded cages. Glittering crystal chandeliers hung from the tent created an elegant glow as the sun set. Round tables set with simple white cloths let the rainbow of colors pop, as did beaded clear glass plates, revealing bright coral napkins beneath. The design is a case study in the power of color and the impact of using vertical space: hanging chandeliers, ribbons, and butterflies from the tall tent ceilings, and using very tall floral arrangements strategically throughout the space directed the eye upward to spark those awe-inspiring moments.

Many couples who get married at Ocean House have a personal connection to the area, whether they've grown up there or visited every summer, forming a deep attachment to the place and landscape. The bride, though she grew up in the South, summered on Rhode Island and knew she wanted to get married here, sharing with friends from around the world the magic of New England summers by the shore.

OPPOSITE: Love is in the air: crystal chandeliers, twenty thousand yards of multicolored ribbons, and hundreds of butterflies completely transformed the sailcloth tent from the top down. FOLLOWING SPREAD: The brilliant color palette extended to the floral centerpieces and coral napkins.

ABOVE: Brightly hued, full-blown roses, peonies, ranunculuses, and other garden blossoms spilled out of gilded birdcages for enchanting centerpieces. OPPOSITE: Butterflies in flight, alluding to how the couple met on a delayed plane flight, alighted on the cake and centerpieces, and cascaded in drifts across the tent ceiling.

ABOVE, FROM LEFT: Escort cards with elegant butterfly motifs were clipped to a wooden window-frame screen; they corresponded to table numbers framed in moss. High-top cocktail tables were draped in bright coral-pink fabric wrapped with an ivy garland. For the rehearsal dinner, escort cards were tucked into a wall of boxwood greenery. FOLLOWING SPREAD: The tent, on the lawn between the Ocean House and the actual ocean, was illuminated romantically as the sun set.

GREAT IDEAS FOR COLORFUL WEDDINGS

- Let your imagination take flight. What sounds like the simplest of motifs—butterflies—was interpreted for this wedding couple in creative and captivating ways that were sophisticated, not kitschy. Think of a theme or motif that might symbolize your relationship, background, interests, or the locale and spark a unique approach to your decor.
- Take an idea and fly with it. A simple material—ribbon—is transporting when strung in multicolors across the entire ceiling, transforming a basic white tent.
- Don't be afraid of color. The bright pinks, oranges, and yellows here were offset by simple white dotted Swiss tablecloths, natural wood chairs, and greenery.

AUBERGE DU SOLEIL

RUTHERFORD, CALIFORNIA

A Spectacular Vintage

Perched on sunlit rolling hills in fabled Napa Valley, Auberge du Soleil pairs breathtaking scenery with world-renowned cuisine and wines.

OPPOSITE: A bride and groom enjoyed an intimate moment in the picturesque allée of the olive grove. This beautiful hideaway is home to a sculpture garden, meditative stream, and scented lavender. FOLLOWING SPREAD: Most weddings take place on the Ceremony Terrace, with captivating views of Napa Valley.

Nestled amidst a thirty-three-acre olive grove in Napa Valley, Northern California's famed vineyard region, Auberge du Soleil began as Napa's first fine-dining restaurant in 1981. It was the dream of French restaurateur Claude Rouas, who envisioned creating an inn and gourmet restaurant reminiscent of Provence in an area equally as breathtaking, but at the time, not nearly as well-known. Five years later, Rouas and his partner, Bob Harmon, created the inn—a series of enchanting small "maisons" perched across the hillside, sited to take in the spectacular views and provide privacy.

Forty years later, Auberge du Soleil continues to win Michelin stars and is still considered one of the most inviting luxury resorts in the world. It's hard to imagine a more transporting setting for weddings. Whether you're having an intimate ceremony on the outdoor terrace with breathtaking views of the entire valley, or a petite wedding in the sculpture garden beneath the canopy of century-old olive trees, or in the Japanese *ryokan*-inspired, open-air pavilion, nature plays a starring role in any celebration here. "Eighty percent of the time we have good weather," notes Jamie Lagoyda, Auberge du Soleil's wedding planner, "but even on a foggy afternoon, with the olive trees and evergreens shimmering in the mist, it has a whole other layer of romance." Auberge du Soleil may have started the trend, but now many couples enjoy hosting weddings at wineries, which are almost always situated in beautiful countryside. It's proof that when you have such a spectacular setting, there's very little else you need to do to wow your guests. The sculpture garden and Japanese pavilion offer equally inspired ideas for enchanting venues as well.

Incredible meals and excellent wines are at the heart of the Napa Valley experience, and weddings at Auberge du Soleil fully capitalize on these specialties, under the direction of Executive Chef Robert Curry. The layout also offers ease of movement between indoors and out, a plus to keep in mind for any wedding. The ceremony, cocktails, and hors d'oeuvres often take place outside on the terrace, with everyone then coming indoors for a multicourse,

OPPOSITE: Sheltered beneath a rustic chuppah, a couple shared a kiss after their ceremony.

sit-down gourmet dinner. After dinner, guests might move back outdoors to indulge in mini desserts and a nightcap, gathered around the firepit beneath a blanket of stars.

Wines are an essential part of the meals here, and the sommelier can arrange for wine pairings or tastings from the area or any region, drawing on Auberge du Soleil's expertly curated fifteen-thousand-bottle cellar. One couple hosted a "tour de monde" tasting featuring their favorite wines from travels around the globe, which were highlighted on a map. Another standout experience Auberge du Soleil offers is a custom champagne sabering. The sommelier teaches the couple how to saber, or slice the cork off, a bottle of champagne before the wedding, so they can add this dramatic gesture to the toasts. The olive-wood-handled saber is monogrammed with their names and the wedding date, and presented in a keepsake olive-wood box. For anyone daring enough to try it, sabrage adds a touch of showmanship to any wedding. But you needn't risk an accident to give a toast that will make your wedding memorable.

OPPOSITE: A "petite wedding" ceremony can be set up in Le Jardin, a more intimate spot in the olive grove on the lower part of the property, with a keyhole view of Napa Valley. ABOVE: The sweetest moment: the first married kiss, celebrated with a confetti of flower petals. FOLLOWING SPREAD: A trellis filled with wisteria, what Auberge du Soleil calls a "floral cascade," has dramatic visual and fragrant impact. Lush rose bouquets hold back gauze drapes, creating a sheltering stage for the ceremony.

GREAT IDEAS FOR VINEYARD WEDDINGS

- Host a wine tasting with wines from favorite places you've visited as a couple.
- Learn to saber a champagne bottle (carefully!) for a dramatic toast.
- Fill a trellis or pergola with wisteria, lilac, or other cascading flowers over the ceremony or seating area.
- Serve *croquembouche* instead of a wedding cake, for Parisian flair.

ABOVE: The wedding party enjoyed an exuberant, unscripted moment of joy, after the ceremony. OPPOSITE: The Auberge du Soleil pastry chef created this delectable *croquembouche*, a traditional French confection made with cream puff pastry arranged in a cone shape and joined with spun caramel.

Wedding Cakes

Wedding cakes are always a focal point and a canvas for creativity. The good news is that the cakes now taste as good as they look, with couples opting for "a more natural look and wide range of delicious flavors," notes Enid Drummond, pastry chef for the Post Hotel & Spa. "I've even made cakes with different flavors and fillings for each tier." Here, her pointers, along with wedding cake trends and inspiration:

- Flowers are one of the most popular ways to decorate cakes, but now they're just as likely to be fresh flowers as sugar blossoms. Pressed edible flowers or ferns are on trend as well.
- If you want your cake displayed during the reception, especially on a warm day, soft icings like buttercream aren't a good idea. Consider something sturdier like ganache or refrigerate the cake once everyone's had a chance to see it.
- Other appealing new looks for wedding cakes include watercolor-like painting on cakes; precise geometric and tile patterns; metallic accents such as gold or bronze; textured or embossed white-on-white cakes; ruffled buttercream frosting.
- Some couples are opting for several smaller cakes in different flavors and varied, but coordinated, decoration. Single-tier and square cakes are also gaining favor, as well as individual cakes.
- One semi-controversial trend that Drummond endorses is the "naked" or "semi-naked" cake, which is lightly iced so that some of the cake shows through (some icing is good to help keep the cake moist).
- Some people are offering dessert buffets instead of cakes or even serving "cakes" made of doughnuts or wheels of cheese.

RIGHT AND OPPOSITE: From highly realistic sugar blossoms to real flowers, leaves, and berries, florals are a timeless, always-right choice for wedding cakes. Buttercream ruffles and metallic and geometric designs look fresh as well.

AUBERGE SAINT-ANTOINE

QUÉBEC CITY, QUÉBEC, CANADA

A Window on the Past

On an archaeological site steeped in centuries of history, Auberge Saint-Antoine melds museum and hotel, and contemporary design with a reverence for the past.

OPPOSITE: The bride and groom shared a toast and tête-à-tête at their November wedding. His burgundy tuxedo and boutonniere hinted at the autumnal palette of the reception, while her simple yet elegant gown provided modern contrast to the centuries-old setting.

In the heart of Québec City's Old Port, overlooking the St. Lawrence River, Auberge Saint-Antoine provides a portal to the past intertwined with modern-day urban luxury. The three-building site has borne witness to four hundred years of history as a wharf, cannon battery, and maritime warehouse. When the hotel was being constructed in the early 1990s, and when it was renovated and expanded in 2003, an archaeological dig on site unearthed over five thousand artifacts, some dating back to the 1600s. More than eight hundred of those artifacts are now artfully displayed throughout the hotel, including the guest rooms, creating what is truly a living museum. This careful balance of old and new celebrates the past while also anchoring the hotel very much in the present. The original 1822 warehouse's stone walls and wooden beams have been preserved and are on display in the restaurant, Chez Muffy, and the event space, while much of the interior design is decidedly contemporary, and modern comforts abound.

Small-scale weddings of ninety or fewer guests are hosted in a private dining room in the 1822 warehouse, where sails for schooners were once repaired. The thick plaster walls, centuries-old wooden floors, posts, and beams are all original, and the stout ropes that serve as informal railings nod to the space's maritime past. "You can feel the history in this space," says Dagmar Lombard, the *Maître de Maison*. "It's not your typical soulless ballroom. It tells a story." By virtue of the room's size and historic charm, weddings here have an inviting intimacy.

For the November wedding pictured here, the emphasis was on neutral, earthy colors and natural materials that complemented the pronounced textures of the well-aged wood and plaster in the room. Hand-loomed linen, wicker, wood, and pewter, and natural foliage and dried grasses felt of a piece with the setting. The hand-calligraphed and printed invitations on deckle-edge handmade paper perfectly suited the site and the event, and included a

OPPOSITE: The invitation suite's aged, handcrafted feel is evocative of the location. The loose, artistic calligraphy; the charming pen-and-ink illustration of Auberge Saint-Antoine; the handmade, deckle-edge paper; and the hand-dyed silk ribbon that tied together all the elements created a sense of anticipation for the event and a beautiful keepsake.

MAGYAR
1960
names
accepts
declines
Marie-Camille & Baptiste are getting married!
october the twelfth
two thousand and nineteen
Quebec City, Canada
formal invitation to follow
Rehearsal Dinner
CHEZ MUFFY
10 rue saint-antoine
Brunch

charming pen-and-ink illustration of the hotel and leafy garlands encircling the RSVP card. Flowers in a muted, autumnal palette of ivory, tan, peach, and rust, mixed with pussy willows, leafy branches, wheat, seedpods, fruits, and other foraged fare emphasized natural textures and the beauty of the harvest. Hand-dyed silk ribbons tied around the invitations, napkins, and bouquets; gauzy, layered linen tablecloths; and candles in pumpkin and ivory hues echoed the tonal palette with subtle sophistication.

The sit-down dinner featured the excellent farm-to-fork fare and the late-season bounty of the hotel's large vegetable farm on Île d'Orléans. Afterwards, guests moved to the adjacent Hall Explore for music and dancing.

This historic neighborhood of Old Québec, with its cobblestone streets and Parisian flavor, make it an irresistibly romantic spot for weddings within a sophisticated, cosmopolitan city.

OPPOSITE, FROM LEFT: Bouquets and boutonnieres featuring flowers, grasses, and foliage in shades of pale peach, ivory, wheat, and rust complement the natural setting as well as the season. The menus were created by the same calligrapher as the invitations.

GREAT IDEAS FOR HISTORIC WEDDING SITES

- Give your invitations an old-world feel with deckle-edge paper and incorporate calligraphy and illustrations in the design.
- Centuries-old buildings lend a great deal of atmosphere without any extra adornment, thanks to their architecture and timeless materials.
- Use natural linen, wood, wicker, and pewter to add textural richness to table settings.
- A trio of smaller cakes, rather than one large one, feels fresh, and allows you to offer different flavors.

ABOVE AND OPPOSITE: In Canada, it is often customary for the bride and groom to sit at their own "sweetheart" table so they can have a few private moments of conversation amidst all the celebration, and this *table à deux* became a distillation of the naturally elegant decor. Layered linen tablecloths complemented the rough-hewn plaster walls, and wooden candlesticks echoed the centuries-old, wide-plank wooden warehouse floors. Woven in among the flowers are pears, pussy willows, seedpods, and autumn leaves, evoking the foraged beauty of a walk in the woods.

ABOVE: Each place setting was layered atop a bleached wicker charger, with a small posy placed on the napkin. The place cards were written in calligraphy on pale shells. OPPOSITE: A trio of smaller wedding cakes is a refreshing alternative to one large one (and also allows more flavor options); each was adorned with sugar flowers resembling dogwood blossoms in the same monochrome hues. Vintage gilded wood trays were used to serve cocktails and form a backdrop for a photograph of the wedding rings.

LAS MAÑANITAS

CUERNAVACA, MEXICO

Tropical Paradise

Surrounded by lush gardens with exotic birds and perfect weather year-round, you will feel transported to paradise, a perfect place for a wedding.

OPPOSITE: Many Mexican weddings feature a bride and groom's table like this one. The ornately carved table, set up on the patio with fountains behind it, was lavished with white flowers. A large tree hung with candlelit glass lanterns created a romantic backdrop.

Thanks to its ideal warm and sunny climate, Cuernavaca, Mexico, about an hour south of Mexico City, is known as the "city of eternal spring." Strolling the grounds of Las Mañanitas, you sense that this motto could also be attributed to the overwhelming abundance of flowers. The five acres of lush, immaculately maintained gardens that surround Las Mañanitas create a verdant refuge dotted with exotic birds such as African crested cranes, traditional and albino peacocks, macaws, and parrots as well as sculptures by noted Mexican artist Francisco Zúñiga. Las Mañanitas is known as much for its gardens and gourmet restaurant as its hotel, an elegant, old-world hacienda with twenty-seven spacious suites decorated in traditional Mexican colonial style.

Celebrating the region's cultural and historic heritage, the food of Chef Etny Molina at Las Mañanitas is focused on traditional Mexican specialties and ancestral recipes using fresh local ingredients and served on handmade pottery that showcases native craft traditions.

For the springtime wedding of the daughter of the owners, Francisco and Rebeca Bernot, no detail was overlooked. Lorenza had recently vacationed in Italy and wanted to conjure the sunny, fragrant beauty of the Amalfi coast for her wedding, enlisting citrus trees, lemons, and vibrant yellow flowers that were woven throughout the gardens and reception. "Normally we use the covered terrace for dining in case of rain, but my sister didn't want a tent or roof of any kind. She wanted to be outdoors, see the sky, and feel like you were eating in the garden," recalls her brother Diego Bernot, head of finance for the family business. "Spring is the most beautiful time here, when everything is in bloom,

OPPOSITE: In the gardens of Las Mañanitas, the existing, beautiful old stone planters and flower beds are enhanced with flowers chosen by each bride, like these white blossoms and branches.

RIGHT: Other brides and grooms choose to sit at a long table with their families, like this one for twenty members of the Bernot clan and the groom's family, beneath the sheltering floral canopy of *lluvia de oro*, or "golden shower," trees. Yellow and white flower arrangements were even nestled between tree boughs. Flowerpots of tulips and fresh herbs brightened the tables, while underneath, leaves and lemons created a verdant screen.

GREAT IDEAS FOR TROPICAL WEDDINGS

- Take inspiration from a place you've traveled to and bring its style to your own wedding. Here, the lemons and citrus trees of the Amalfi coast inspired the palette, decor, and menu.
- Use flowerpots with fresh herbs as both decoration and help-yourself seasoning for the meal.
- Take advantage of trees in bloom and other garden elements to effortlessly enhance your own floral decoration.
- Give paper parasols to guests or hang them above a terrace to provide shelter from the sun.
- Use small trees and topiaries as decor that can live on after the wedding.
- Check weather records going back five or more years to see what the typical temperatures and rainfall averages are for dates you're considering for your wedding.

and she studied the weather records going back ten or fifteen years and determined that it hadn't ever rained on that date in March." According to Diego, three hundred people is a "small" Mexican wedding; the Bernots hosted eight hundred guests at a sit-down dinner for their daughter's wedding.

The stunning beauty of the gardens was enhanced by spectacular floral cascades across tables, lemon topiaries and centerpieces, and lavish yellow-and-white bouquets, which echoed the naturally flowering canopy of the *lluvia de oro*, or "golden shower" trees overhead, with long clusters of sunny blossoms dripping from their branches. A dramatic flower-draped pergola erected across the dining terrace created a similar effect, particularly eye-catching when it was lit up at night. After a night of dining, dancing, and dining some more, the last guests finally left at about 4 a.m., the sign of a truly enchanting celebration.

OPPOSITE, FROM LEFT: With so many tables, taking a varied approach to the tablescapes was appealing and refreshing. Every fifth table or so was decorated with a lavish and dramatic cascade of flowers spilling over the end of the table. Others had simpler bowls of lemons and leaves, and pots of herbs such as basil and thyme that could be pinched off to season the food. Topiary trees with lemons and conventional floral bouquets decorated still other tables, giving them all a sunny exuberance. FOLLOWING SPREAD: Many guests were seated for dinner in the garden itself, where a floor was laid down to protect the grass. A tall pergola was constructed using all-natural materials, and dramatically lit to showcase the flowers. Candlelit tables and lighting throughout the gardens created a warm, inviting glow.

18

ABOVE AND OPPOSITE: For two other weddings, all the flowers were classic, elegant white, which complemented the lush greenery. One had white rose petals strewn along the aisle leading to the flower-crowned altar. Globes of white flowers on bamboo tripods marked the rows of seating. For the other ceremony, an extravagance of white roses decorated the altar and posts along the aisle, which was covered by a white platform.

ABOVE: In a seating area extending out from the terrace, white paper parasols were hung from cables to help filter the sun. Mirrored tabletops and place mats reflected the beauty of the trees, flowers, and sky onto the tables. White flower arrangements in tall candelabras created dramatic centerpieces. OPPPOSITE: Waterfalls, fountains, and a koi pond create the soothing sound of water throughout the gardens. A tall, moss-draped topiary tree was adorned with white orchids, with white roses at its base, for a sumptuous natural centerpiece that seamlessly connected with the garden setting.

55

MAGEE HOMESTEAD

SARATOGA, WYOMING

Unbridled Luxury

For authentic Western adventure leavened with luxury, look no further than Magee Homestead, a century-old working cattle ranch set on thirty thousand acres of breathtaking scenery in Wyoming's Platte River Valley.

OPPOSITE: A newly married couple walked across a wide-open pasture at Magee Homestead, a symbolic start to the journey of their new life together, with the Sierra Madre and Snow Mountains in the distance.

Under endless Wyoming skies, backed by the dramatic peaks of the Rockies and rooted in the authentic heritage of the American West, Magee Homestead, part of a working cattle ranch, hosts highly personalized, indelible destination weddings. Its private lodge and collection of nine restored historic log cabins, which housed cowboys starting in the late 1880s, blend rustic, casual ease with plush accommodations. For those who like riding horses or fly-fishing by day and cozying up by a campfire at night, or prefer blue jeans and cowboy boots to black tie, a Western wedding in a jaw-dropping setting is a slice of heaven. A ranch wedding automatically feels more relaxed, and offers a special opportunity to share a whole weekend full of activities with friends and family—from sunrise hikes and yoga to a trail ride or shooting practice—at an all-inclusive luxury ranch in a setting your guests won't soon forget.

Magee Homestead is an exclusive Relais & Châteaux property hosting just twenty-nine guests, but with full use of the larger Brush Creek Ranch property, which offers the best of both worlds—individualized attention and world-class cuisine, along with a wide variety of activities and settings to take advantage of across the 7,500-acre property. Weddings here have the entire Homestead to themselves. Guests can partake in guided outdoor activities at the ranch and in the beautiful Medicine Bow National Forest, then meet up for campfires and chuckwagon cookouts—but they can also enjoy gourmet meals, spa treatments, and wine tastings or dinners in the ninety-four-yard wine tunnel. Menus feature American Black Wagyu cattle raised on the ranch, organic fruits and vegetables grown in the hydroponic greenhouses, and farm-made delicacies from the on-site creamery, bakery, distillery, and brewery, all under the direction of Executive Chef Ülfet Ralph.

In a setting like Magee, open only from late May through October, couples naturally want to host their weddings outdoors to take full advantage of the spectacular scenery (though

OPPOSITE: Weddings at Magee Homestead have use of the full Brush Creek Ranch property, including this dramatic overlook at Falcon Peak, at about seven thousand feet elevation, with views of the Sierra Madre Mountains and the valley below, for a spectacular setting for a ceremony, meal, or even a yoga class.

tents and indoor backup plans are always available). Weddings are necessarily on the smaller side, so family and friends can enjoy a long weekend's worth of activities together. Meals might be anything from a prairie supper in the pasture to a gourmet dinner in the wine cellar. "You can develop the menus with the chef and we can entirely customize it with bonfires, fireworks, anything," says proprietor Jeremy Belnap. A ranch wedding transports you and your guests to a nearly bygone era of the American West, blending pioneering adventure and the great outdoors with unexpected luxury, comfort, and welcoming warmth.

OPPOSITE: The Cheyenne Club, part of Brush Creek Ranch, can be used to host dinners or larger gatherings. ABOVE: A scenic pasture was set up for a wedding ceremony with the addition of wooden pews framed by baskets of all-white flowers and edged in a border of natural grasses.

RIGHT: Gourmet dining, cowboy-style: Blue denim napkins, tied like neckerchiefs and edged in red, picked up on the vibrant red anemones mixed with wildflowers and herbs in the centerpieces, for an outdoor dinner. Riveted wood-handled flatware, galvanized metal chargers, and lanterns set a welcoming down-home table.

GREAT IDEAS FOR RANCH WEDDINGS

- For a destination wedding, plan a full weekend's worth of (optional) activities for guests, from hiking and yoga to welcome dinners and casual lunches, so everyone can meet each other and enjoy all the location has to offer. But be sure to allow for downtime as well.
- Bring people together outdoors for nighttime events with a bonfire or campfire.
- Go all-out Western with bandana or denim napkins, cowhide or shearling-draped chairs, and a casual dress code that welcomes jeans and cowboy boots for informal dinners.

ABOVE: Western luxe: teepee-style tents and sheepskin-draped stools were gathered round a chuckwagon cauldron with a small wood fire for toasting s'mores in cozy warmth. OPPOSITE: Welcome cocktails were set up outside with cocktail tables, comfy cowhide Equipale chairs, and the romantic glow of string lights and candle hurricanes. Denim and cowboy hats are always appropriate.

THE WICKANINNISH INN

TOFINO, BRITISH COLUMBIA, CANADA

Swept Away

On the rugged, windswept coast of Vancouver Island, the untamed beauty of rocky beaches and sheltering cedars sets a dramatic backdrop for intimate celebrations.

OPPOSITE: A couple celebrated their elopement on Chesterman Beach, right outside the Wickaninnish Inn, before enjoying an intimate dinner at The Pointe Restaurant. The inn is perched on the rocky coast, with a front-row view of the exhilarating waves, abundant wildlife, and sparkling ocean.

Even coming from Vancouver, it's a five-hour journey. You take a ferry across to Vancouver Island, and as you drive through the Pacific Rim National Park, "the modern world starts to fall away," explains Charles McDiarmid, the Wickaninnish Inn's managing director, whose family's small cabin still graces this remote treasure. "The last hour and a half of the drive is all rainforest, mountains, rivers, trees, and lakes, maybe even a bear." Literally at the end of the road, the inn sits amidst a hundred acres of land belonging to the McDiarmid family, where old-growth forest meets the rocky coast of the Pacific Ocean, near the tiny town of Tofino, known for surfing and storm-watching.

In the mid-1990s, the McDiarmid family built an inn designed to harmonize with the natural landscape, using local cedar, fir, driftwood, and stone. Each room is positioned for panoramic views of the seascape, with large windows that make you feel one with the view. From the hand-carved front doors and hand-adzed posts and beams by master carver Henry Nolla to the signature driftwood chairs, each room features the handiwork, sculpture, and artwork of local artisans.

"For weddings, we attract couples looking for something unique and off the beaten path," (literally), says Megan Jones, special events manager. "It's casual, yet high-end—it's about kicking off your shoes and walking in the sand, but also relishing the gourmet meals. Everything is kept as natural as possible, and you feel secluded in

RIGHT: A just-wed couple enjoyed a private moment in the sanctuary beneath towering, centuries-old Western red cedars. "These giants have never been touched by a logger's chainsaw or axe," explains Charles McDiarmid. "It has a primal feeling, like Stonehenge."

your own private hideaway." Wedding celebrations on an intimate scale—no more than sixty people—take place on the inn's private Shell Beach, which is tucked away at the end of a trail winding through the old-growth forest. Marquee tents, set up on the beach just for weddings, shelter long tables made of live-edge cedar with tree stumps for seating. Ceremonies can also be held in a magical forest clearing, beneath a natural cathedral of two-hundred-foot-tall, centuries-old spruce, hemlock, and Western red cedars. After the rainforest ceremony, guests walk to Shell Beach for dinner. Executive Chef Carmen Ingham and his team prepare the food right on the beach, explaining to guests about the fresh-caught whole roasted salmon, Dungeness crab, British Columbia beef tenderloin, and locally grown grilled vegetables.

Couples who wed here want to take advantage of the outdoors, and the inn can organize whale-watching expeditions, sea kayaking, salmon fishing, nature walks or hikes, paddleboarding, and more. "Our theme is 'rustic elegance on nature's edge,'" says McDiarmid, and that's a perfect description of their very personalized weddings as well.

OPPOSITE AND ABOVE: Wedding dinners and receptions take place on Shell Beach, a private beach owned by the inn, where alcoholic drinks can be served, bonfires built, and dancing and celebrating can go on until the wee hours. All wedding cakes are created in-house by the pastry team. This naked-style carrot cake with buttercream frosting and a caramel drizzle was adorned with natural ferns and blossoms. This beautiful bride chose a naturalistic bouquet leafed with ferns, wildflowers, and roses.

ABOVE: A couple walked beneath the hand-adzed timbers of the port cochère outside the Pointe Building, on the way to their reception at Shell Beach.
OPPOSITE: A bird's-eye view of Wickaninnish Inn shows The Pointe Restaurant in front, with the Beach Building hidden in the trees behind it. To the right is Chesterman Beach, and at the far left, you can see a tiny edge of Shell Beach—a path leads from the inn through the forest to reach it. Virgin forest, meandering waterways, and the mountains rise behind it in this remote, unspoiled setting on the far western Pacific coast of British Columbia.

GREAT IDEAS FOR RUSTIC WEDDINGS

- For a casual outdoor wedding or rehearsal dinner, consider having the food cooked on the spot to make the food preparation interactive and hot-off-the-grill fresh.
- Have your cake reflect the environment, with a tree-trunk platter, leafy ferns and flowers, or shells adorning your cake.
- Advise guests of the terrain, so they know to bring shoes that are appropriate for the beach, rugged ground, or walking.

ABOVE: A bride and groom emerged from the Rainforest Beach Trail into the unspoiled beauty of Chesterman Beach. OPPOSITE: A simple but delectable wedding cake, made by the Wickaninnish Inn pastry chef, was crowned with beachcombing finds of mussel and scallop shells, with a watercolor border that evoked sea-sprayed waves.

Just Married
9.10.11

WINVIAN FARM

MORRIS, CONNECTICUT

Storybook Fantasy

Colonial Connecticut meets architectural whimsy in this one-of-a-kind resort, where unique cottages let you live out your fantasies of staying in a tree house, lighthouse, even a helicopter—or just hosting a beautiful wedding.

OPPOSITE: This mint-condition vintage truck is perfectly in keeping with the historic and agrarian spirit of Winvian Farm. The bride and groom rented it for their short ride from the ceremony to the reception, and for some picturesque photos.

Have you ever wished you could sleep in a tree house? Bunk in a lighthouse? Or even a beaver's den? Winvian Farm is a place to indulge your childhood fantasies or rather, the most luxurious versions of them. Centered on an original 1775 Colonial home and barn and spread across more than a hundred acres are eighteen architecturally distinct cottages that let your imagination take flight. Winvian is a place that inspires whimsical and creative weddings as well as more traditional and refined ones. One magazine aptly described it as "113 acres of Norman Rockwell meets *Alice in Wonderland*."

In the Camping Cottage, for example, forest murals grace the walls, the bed lies beneath a tented canopy, there are indoor and outdoor fireplaces, and the vaulted ceiling is illuminated with stars at night. The Treehouse may be suspended thirty-five feet above the ground, but it's outfitted with unexpected luxuries like gas fireplaces, a steam shower and Jacuzzi, and a full bar. And another dwelling features a fully restored 1968 Sikorsky Coast Guard helicopter inside, with a mod bar and lounge inside the chopper, and a king-size bed and Jacuzzi tub in the cottage.

Set against the backdrop of eighteenth-century buildings and the gardens, fields, and rolling hills of Litchfield County, Connecticut, weddings here can also be quite elegant and luxurious. "Our whole philosophy is to provide an environment where guests can create anything they want their wedding to be, whether they want an intimate elopement or a three-hundred-person extravaganza," says Winvian president Heather Smith. Winvian has hosted everything from a creative circus-themed wedding to a gala celebration inside a

OPPOSITE: Joy ride: the groom, center, and his groomsmen pedaled the resort's bikes from their various cottages to the wedding ceremony. FOLLOWING SPREAD: This bride and groom took time for a private walk after their ceremony along the gardens at the organic farm. The cottages visible from the road have red barnlike exteriors that hide their fanciful interiors; here, Helicopter and Charter Oak.

CHARTER OAK
WINVIAN

glass box built just for the night to a wedding that transformed the barn into a disco lounge with white leather couches, white-draped walls, and glitter balls. "And we also have many people who say 'I love the barn how it is, I just want lots of candles and wildflowers from the gardens, and that's it.' No matter what, we try to make each couple's vision come to life," says Smith.

Weddings here are designed to showcase the bucolic scenery, the historic buildings, and the exceptional food, under the direction of Executive Chef Chris Eddy. Ceremonies often take place outside the 1775 Seth Bird House, overlooking the gardens and organic farm. Receptions are typically hosted in the Gordon Brown House, a large, rustic barn with adjacent terraces, or in a sailcloth tent on a level field in the center of the property. Many weddings become weekend-long events that encompass all the property has to offer, including a pool, spa, biking, nature walks, and other activities. Hosts often organize a strolling welcome party among the various cottages where guests are staying, so people can get a peek at all the eclectic and amazing lodgings. Different cocktails and appetizers are served at each cottage on the tour, an invitingly interactive idea that could just as easily be adapted to hotel rooms or villas. Winvian can arrange everything from hot air balloon rides to bonfires, and the surrounding area offers activities like golf, tennis, canoeing, and fishing. "Even for guests who live in Connecticut, it becomes like a destination wedding without having to get on a plane," says Smith. "The property itself is such a special place that to have it all to themselves is just magical."

OPPOSITE: This bride's stunning yet understated beaded dress and bouquet showcase simple sophistication: lush peonies are surrounded by green mist, deutzia, and greenery. FOLLOWING SPREAD: A naturalistic chuppah crafted from tree limbs is perfectly suited to the forested backdrop.

ABOVE: The Gordon Brown House barn can be completely opened up to the terrace, which can be tented, as it is here, to accommodate more guests. OPPOSITE: You can never go wrong with timeless classics. Echoing the bride's bouquet, simple elegance carried through to the reception where mercury glass vases held white peonies and alliums, sweetheart roses, and viburnums, on white tablecloths with simple white taper candles.

WOODLAND ENCHANTMENT

For a Broadway actor and a musical director, a love of gardening, great food, and nature made Winvian an ideal setting for their August wedding. Wildflowers, woodland blooms, succulents, and ferns were nestled in beds of moss; tumbled from rustic galvanized vases and glass terrariums; and were even spiked on wooden blocks, creating a richly hued tapestry of colors and textures. The vibrant and unexpected centerpieces created the feeling of dining in a magical forest. Simple, natural linen table runners beneath the place settings let the flowers take center stage on wooden farmhouse tables. The grooms were married beneath a chuppah crafted from tree limbs woven with a profusion of sunflowers, wildflowers, and greenery. Escort cards to guide guests to their tables were planted in flowerpots of mini succulents atop a table carpeted with moss. A creative approach to every detail, even the grooms' attire, suffused the entire celebration.

OPPOSITE: After a ceremony that blended Jewish traditions with Eastern spirituality, beneath a natural chuppah, or wedding canopy, the grooms both broke the glass. This Jewish ritual is meant to symbolize the destruction of the temples and the frailty of human relationships, but also a wish that the marriage should never shatter.

ABOVE AND OPPOSITE: Outside the 1775 Seth Bird House, the main house and restaurant, a moss-draped table holds tiny flowerpots filled with succulents and the guests' names and table numbers. After the ceremony, the cocktail hour was held on this terrace, then guests moved to the barn and patio for the reception. Guests could write their well-wishes for the couple in a photo book as a meaningful alternative to simply signing a guest book.

GREAT IDEAS FOR WOODLAND WEDDINGS

- As an alternative to traditional centerpieces, create woodland-inspired arrangements with wildflowers and ferns. Fashion in staggered heights and loose, naturalistic arrangements to mimic how flowers grow in the wild.
- Cover tables in moss for serving food, holding place cards, or as part of the centerpieces.
- Use mini terra-cotta pots with flowers or succulents for charming escort card holders.
- For an outdoor wedding, have your florist build an altar or chuppah using tree limbs and flowers.
- Instead of tablecloths, lay linen runners beneath plates to show off wooden tables for a more natural, modern look.
- Host a progressive welcome cocktail party in various rooms or homes on the first night that guests arrive to encourage mingling.
- Use a photo book with pictures of the couple as a guest book.

OPPOSITE AND ABOVE: A lively mix of dahlias, thistles, ferns, cockscombs, orchids, freesias, wildflowers, succulents, seedpods, and much more were arranged naturalistically in fluted metal, stone, and wooden planters down the center of each table. Some tables featured small beds of moss or glass terrariums, while others had larger, shallow stone planters, giving each table its own individual, eclectic feel, as in nature. Nothing was "matching." Simple glass votives and lanterns were nestled around the arrangements.

CLASSIC ELEGANCE

For an early summer wedding charmed with perfect weather, this bride and groom celebrated with the classics, from pale pink and white roses to elegant china and silver—proof that timeless elegance is always in style. Interestingly, when the owners of Winvian began hosting weddings, they chose not to provide standard tables, chairs, and china, knowing their guests would most likely want to put their own individual stamp on each event. They work with a number of rental companies to provide a wide range of unique and personalized choices for the table settings. In the case of this wedding, the tables were set with heirloom-inspired floral-banded china mixed with more modern beaded glass chargers and blush vintage-style cut-glass champagne coupes. Mixing and matching different types of china and glassware will give your wedding a more personal feel, as if you were hosting it in your home. Some couples also choose to collect or borrow vintage china or silver to use for their table settings and centerpieces. Matched with abundant flowers in a palette of white, pink, and purple, this is a wedding look for all seasons.

OPPOSITE: This bride's stunning dress, featuring embroidered ripples of abstract blossoms, stood out against the towering evergreens. This long stone walkway between the spa and the main building is a favorite spot for photos.

ABOVE: The blush hue of the bridesmaids' dresses is echoed in their bouquets of pink and white roses, dahlias, and hydrangeas with accents of deeper red roses. The flower girl wore a charming fresh floral headband and posy. OPPOSITE: A modern approach to florals is to create bouquets of a single type of flower grouped together. Here, bouquets from delicate lacecap hydrangeas to petite spray roses have been placed in clear glass vases of different heights. While Winvian generally does not serve buffet style in order to control the quality and temperature of food, they will serve desserts and charcuterie boards on tables where guests can help themselves.

RIGHT: Simply stunning: A mix of round and rectangular tables, some with tablecloths and others left bare, is layered with floral-banded china on beaded glass chargers, with clear wineglasses and pale pink, pressed-glass goblets that catch the streaming sunlight. Lush centerpieces pair white garden roses with purple buddleia and sweet peas.

Place Settings

Table settings don't have to default to white. With the range of rental services today, you can create a more personalized look that carries your design scheme through to every element. Elizabeth Goslee, events manager at Winvian Farm, offers advice:

- We start with the color scheme of the wedding, the style of the wedding gown and bridesmaid dresses, and what the flowers and invitations will look like, if the couple has chosen those already.
- It's very helpful to see everything set up to judge whether all the elements work together. When couples come in for their tasting, the florist will ideally bring a mockup of the centerpiece, and we'll start making tableware selections.
- Keep in mind that you'll have eight to twelve of each place setting on the table, plus flowers and candles, so you don't want to go too overboard.
- I usually suggest starting with a neutral tablecloth and then choosing one or two elements that will pop. Or sometimes we'll add pattern, say, on the high-top tablecloths for the cocktail hour.
- We start from the bottom up, with tables and chairs, then consider tablecloths and napkins, then china, silverware, glassware, and chargers. About half the couples choose to add chargers for another layer of pattern or texture.
- We require place cards for each guest at the table. This helps speed table service, so waiters know what entrée each person is having, and where to serve special meals for vegan guests or those with allergies.

RIGHT AND OPPOSITE: Think of the table in layers, from the tablecloth and plates to the menu, place card, and napkin ring. Flowers, candles, and even favors, like this rolled-up striped lobster bib, all play a part in the look. You can layer textures of white or choose something eye-catching like a scenic toile or modern metallic dots.

Juliette

THE IVY HOTEL

BALTIMORE, MARYLAND

City Savoir Faire

In this sumptuously decorated jewel of a nineteenth-century mansion in the historic heart of Baltimore, live out your fantasy of marrying in Gilded Age splendor.

OPPOSITE: For a winter wedding, snow was the icing on the cake. Monogrammed duck boots (worn in transit) and a leather jacket added charm and a bit of an edge to the bride's lacy wedding gown. Her seasonal bouquet incorporated bright red berries, evergreens, magnolia leaves, and boxwood.

A wedding in a historic house or mansion can offer elegance, a sense of history, and also the feeling of getting married at home—albeit at one a little grander than your own home. The Ivy Hotel is just such a place. With only eighteen luxurious rooms and suites, this historic mansion has a scale that's both intimate and majestic. Built in 1889 for a prosperous Baltimore industrialist, the meticulously renovated building preserves all its original, glorious detail while encompassing every modern amenity, from a magnificent central staircase lined with stained-glass windows to twenty-three fireplaces (one in each guest room), intricately detailed wood moldings, and inlaid wood floors. Its ornately appointed rooms include a wood-paneled library, plant-filled conservatory, billiards room, and beautiful outdoor courtyard, not to mention a celebrated restaurant and spa. It maintains the spirit of a home because each of its spacious bedrooms is decorated uniquely. Many personal touches at this all-inclusive hotel contribute to the feeling that it is, indeed, your home to enjoy.

This highly personalized attention holds true for weddings as well. The Ivy can provide everything from flowers to the cake to an officiant, and coordinate the details. Weddings here are generally small, with a maximum of sixty guests in the courtyard or indoors. Many couples opt to have their ceremony in the courtyard (which can be tented) and dinner indoors, and sometimes move back outdoors for dancing. "The courtyard is very serene—rare for a city location—in a protected space in the middle of the hotel hushed by ivy-covered walls. It's like city meets historical landmark meets secret garden," says Anna Connors, sales and events manager. And while many couples choose spring-to-fall weddings, a city wedding can feel equally elegant in winter or inclement weather. Holiday decorations and a blanket of snow only add to the romance of a winter wedding. The Ivy even has its own 1960s London black cab for a sophisticated getaway (and great photos).

OPPOSITE, ABOVE AND BELOW: The Ivy owns a vintage 1963 London cab for the bride and groom to make a fashionable getaway. "Since it's pretty old, we always have a backup plan, but it's great for photos," says sales and events manager Anna Connors. Guests sent off the happy couple with white balloons instead of birdseed at the hotel entrance.

THE IVY HOTEL
WLU 131G

In warmer months, a courtyard ceremony provides a sense of privacy and sheltering intimacy. At any time, the advantage of a smaller wedding at a very fine restaurant is that the food and the meal are a highlight of the event, not simply standard-issue fare. Chesapeake Bay and Maryland specialties like crab cakes, oysters, and pit beef are often featured, along with the freshest farmers' market bounty, reflecting both the couples' and chefs' desire to have the food celebrate the best of the locale. A wedding at a hotel like this also offers extra activities to bring people together, like billiards and a piano.

A city location can make it easier for your guests to travel to the wedding, offers many options for the rehearsal dinner, farewell brunch, and more within a walkable radius, and it undoubtedly sparkles with sophistication and energy. When it's in a historic mansion as beautiful as The Ivy, it becomes even more compelling.

GREAT IDEAS FOR CITY WEDDINGS

- Rent a vintage car for your wedding getaway and photo ops.
- Long banquet tables create a feeling of family and community.
- For an unexpected twist, consider monogramming duck boots or high-top sneakers to wear en route to the wedding in case of inclement weather, or to the after-party when your feet are tired. Or have matching pairs made for your bridesmaids or groomsmen as gifts.
- Bridal party photos shot from overhead offer a less-expected vantage point.
- Billiards present a fun late-night activity.

PAGE 218: The array of elegantly appointed rooms in The Ivy feels like a real-life game of Clue. The billiards room features an 18-karat gold-leaf ceiling, a nineteenth-century pool table, and Picasso-inspired murals. It's the perfect spot for a game of pool after the wedding or during a bachelor or bachelorette party. PAGE 219: The wedding party gathered for photos in the snow-dusted courtyard, with fur and leather jackets to ward off the chill. ABOVE AND OPPOSITE: For the editor of a Baltimore weddings magazine who knows every venue in the city, The Ivy was her first choice for an intimate, early fall wedding in the courtyard, with dinner and dancing to a three-piece combo.

OPPOSITE: Long tables outdoors were set simply but elegantly with orchids and all-white flowers, and tall, clear glass hurricanes with white pillar candles, while guests enjoyed a gourmet meal from the hotel's top-rated restaurant, Magdalena. The ivy-covered walls of the courtyard created a lush backdrop, made festive with string lights.

POST HOTEL & SPA

LAKE LOUISE, ALBERTA, CANADA

Winter Wonderland

Set against the spectacular backdrop of the snow-capped Canadian Rockies, the rustic Post Hotel & Spa treats everyone like family and welcomes guests with infectious warmth.

OPPOSITE: A bride and groom embraced on the ice-skating rink, amidst swirling snow and twinkling lights on the towering evergreens, like an enchanted snow globe come to life. FOLLOWING SPREAD: The resort is at its most magical in winter, surrounded by snowcapped pines with the dramatic Fairview Mountain in the background. The chalet-style main lodge is surrounded by riverfront cabins.

In the heart of Banff, Canada's first national park, the Post Hotel is nestled along the Pipestone River with the majestic Rocky Mountains as its postcard-perfect backdrop. The hotel was originally built in 1942 as a rustic ski lodge, but it was purchased in 1978 by the current owners, George and André Schwarz, Swiss brothers and expert ski instructors who taught close by in Lake Louise. Over the past forty-plus years, they have updated and expanded the resort and greatly elevated the cuisine and wine cellar, while preserving the warm hospitality, rustic comforts, and connection to nature the hotel has always celebrated.

Unspoiled natural beauty is the draw here year-round, with hiking, fishing. and whitewater rafting in summer, and excellent skiing, ice-skating, dogsledding, and horse-drawn sleigh rides in winter. But the gourmet cuisine of Swiss Chef Hans Sauter and the award-winning twenty-five-thousand-bottle wine cellar are as compelling as the outdoor activities, and there's no shame in just curling up with a book by the fire or escaping to the spa for the day.

The Post Hotel is proof that winter weddings can be just as magical as those in spring and summer. Weddings here are intimate, personal affairs, often destination events or celebrations with families who have been coming here for decades. What distinguishes the Post Hotel, in addition to the setting, is the highly personalized service. Only one wedding is held per weekend (and none at all during the peak summer months and holidays when the hotel is most busy) and events manager Sabrina Ziegler and the team handle every detail, from arranging flowers to printing menus and place cards to baking the wedding cake.

Ceremonies are often held in the wood-paneled library, with its timbered, vaulted ceiling and massive river-stone fireplace, though they can also be held outside on the banks of the river. "We've even had ceremonies outside on our skating rink—one couple braved five-degree weather

OPPOSITE: A bride's gown was hung from the timbers at Watson House, a three-thousand-square-foot private lodge perched on the banks of the Pipestone River, often rented out by the bride's family or the wedding party as their home base.

RIGHT: Looking straight out of a fairy tale, this wedding party took their photos in front of an ice castle carved on Lake Louise each winter. Picturesque Lake Louise is just a five-minute drive from the Post Hotel by car or shuttle. The bridesmaids' gray velvet gowns fit perfectly with the snowy scenery.

with hot drink stations and homemade marshmallows," says Ziegler. Dinner for up to seventy-two people can be held in the private dining room below the library, and there's even an English-style pub below for late-night drinks and dancing.

"What stands out for me are the weddings that are most personal," says Ziegler. "One couple from Mauritius came for a small destination wedding one December. The day before the wedding, the bride and her family and girlfriends decorated gingerbread houses our pastry chef had made, and then they used them as centerpieces at the wedding dinner." As co-owner George Schwarz notes, "There's a family feeling, a homey feeling here. Many of our staff have been with the hotel for twenty or twenty-five years and know all the families who've been coming here. We're a home away from home."

OPPOSITE: Receptions usually take place in the private dining room, which is bordered on one side with just some of the twenty-five-thousand bottles of wine in their cellar, and covered with white twigs and twinkling fairy lights on the ceiling. The chocolate Eiffel Tower topping a square wedding cake, at left, was handmade by the pastry chef for a couple who got engaged in Paris. ABOVE: The bride and groom played a guessing game with their shoes at this fun and festive reception.

GREAT IDEAS FOR WINTER WEDDINGS

- Consider having a winter or destination wedding in a snowy locale. If you have it around the holidays or New Year's Eve, you can count on beautiful holiday decorations to help with the decor and make it feel more magical.
- Even in winter, look for a beautiful outdoor spot for wedding party photos—it almost always looks prettier than indoors.
- Host your wedding in a library for a less-expected location.
- Use gingerbread houses as centerpieces for a holiday-season wedding.

LEFT: A groom, at right, and his brothers and groomsmen shared a laugh beside the skating rink, with the awe-inspiring backdrop of the Canadian Rockies. On the left is Mount Temple, the highest mountain in the area.

ACKNOWLEDGMENTS

Creating a book is like coordinating a wedding: there's the subject, vision, and planning, all culminating into one big celebration day. Behind every major endeavor is a collective of skilled professionals who illuminate ideas to make them purposeful, tangible, and memorable.

At the helm of a wedding or a major publication is a planner. Brenda Homick served as planner extraordinaire. Like a conductor of a world-class orchestra, Brenda wove together the vision, aesthetic, and editorial demands to create a harmonious work of art. Without her discipline and foresight, this reflection of Relais & Châteaux weddings would have never been created.

The creation of this book would not be possible without Rizzoli publisher Charles Miers and Sandy Gilbert Freidus, who served as senior editor on the project. A publisher is like a venue: an expression of purpose, vision, and execution.

Details of all of the individual weddings were recorded by Jill Simpson, our writer. She was able to translate these celebrations into words. Jill handled these incredibly private moments with care and precision. All successful weddings have contributors who ground the abstract into the tactile: Jill achieved just that.

The overall design and layout were composed by Doug Turshen and Steve Turner. Like all other wedding creatives, these designers capture the wonder of weddings through a collection of photographs and text that speak to the identities of each venue, couple, and the Relais & Châteaux brand.

Thank you to the properties that graciously allowed us to feature their fairy-tale settings. Each destination has perfected the art of the wedding.

Last but certainly not least, thank you to the planners, chefs, staff, florists, photographers, musicians, and designers who assisted with creating dreams into reality. We are forever in awe of the magic curated through your services.

—Daniel Hostettler

OPPOSITE: A couple steals a kiss beneath the majestic Western red cedars of the Wickaninnish Inn.

RELAIS & CHATEAUX

NORTH AMERICA

BERMUDA & THE CARIBBEAN

Calabash Luxury Boutique Hotel
L'Anse Aux Epines
P.O. Box 382
St. George's,
Grenada
+10.473.444.4334

Eden Roc Cap Cana
Boulevard Principal,
Cap Cana
Punta Cana, La Altagracia
23000
Dominican Republic
+1.809.469.7469

Hôtel Le Toiny
Anse de Toiny
Saint Barthélemy
97133
French West Indies
+590.590.27.88.88

Quintessence Hotel
Long Bay
Anguilla
AI-2640
British West Indies
+1.264.498.8106

Rosedon Hotel
61 Pitts Bay Road
Pembroke
HM 08
Bermuda
+1.441.295.1640

Secret Bay
Ross Boulevard
Portsmouth
Dominica
+1.767.445.4444

Tiamo Resort
Driggs Hill
South Andros Island
The Bahamas
+1.786.374.2442

CANADA

Alo Restaurant
163 Spadina Avenue
Toronto, ON
M5V 2L6
416.260.2222

Auberge Saint-Antoine
8 rue Saint-Antoine
Québec, QC
G1K 4C9
888.692.2211

Clayoquot Wilderness Resort
P.O. Box 130
Tofino, BC
V0R 2Z0
250.266.0397

Hastings House Country House Hotel
160 Upper Ganges Road
Salt Spring Island, BC
V8K 2S2
250.537.2362

Langdon Hall Country House
1 Langdon Drive
Cambridge, ON
N3H 4R8
519.740.2100

Manoir Hovey
575 rue Hovey
North Hatley, QC
J0B 2C0
819.842.2421

Post Hotel & Spa
200 Pipestone Road
Lake Louise, AB
T0L 1E0
403.522.3989

Restaurant Europea
1065 rue de la Montagne
Montréal, QC
H3G 0B9
514.398.9229

Sonora Resort
4580 Cowley Crescent
Richmond, BC
V7B 1B8
604.233.0460

Wedgewood Hotel & Spa
845 Hornby Street
Vancouver, BC
V6Z 1V1
604.689.7777

Wickaninnish Inn
Osprey Lane at Chester-man Beach
Tofino, BC
V0R 2Z0
250.725.3100

MEXICO

Hotel Solar de las Ánimas
Calle Ramón Corona #86,
Colonia Centro
Tequila, Jalisco
46400
Mexico
+52.374.742.6700

Imanta Punta de Mita
Montenahuac Lote L
Bahia de Banderas
Higuera Blanca, Nayarit
63734
Mexico
+52.329.298.4200

Las Mañanitas Hotel Garden Restaurant & Spa
Ricardo Linares 107,
Centro
Cuernavaca, Morelos
62000
Mexico
+52.777.362.0000

Pujol
Tennyson 133
Polanco IV Sección
Mexico City
11550
Mexico
+52.555.545.4111

UNITED STATES

Addison Restaurant
5200 Grand Del Mar Way
San Diego, CA
92130
858.314.1900

Auberge du Soleil
180 Rutherford Hill Road
Rutherford, CA
94573
707.963.1211

Bedford Post
954 Old Post Road
Bedford, NY
10506
914.234.7800

Blackberry Farm
1471 West Millers Cove Road
Walland, TN
37886
865.984.8166

Blackberry Mountain
1447 Three Sisters Road
Walland, TN
37886
800.993.7824

Blair Hill Inn
351 Lily Bay Road
Greenville, ME
04441
207.695.0224

Blantyre
16 Blantyre Road
Lenox, MA
01240
413.637.3556

Camden Harbour Inn
83 Bayview Street
Camden, ME
04843
207.236.4200

Canlis
2576 Aurora Avenue North
Seattle, WA
98109
206.283.3313

Canoe Bay
W16065 Hogback Road
Chetek, WI
54728
715.924.4594

Castle Hill Inn
590 Ocean Drive
Newport, RI
02840
401.849.3800

Château du Sureau
48688 Victoria Lane
Oakhurst, CA
93644
559.683.6860

Chatham Inn
359 Main Street
Chatham, MA
02633
508.945.9232

Daniel
60 East 65th Street
New York, NY
10065
212.288.0033

Dunton Hot Springs
52068 Road 38
Dolores, CO
81323
970.882.4800

Eleven Madison Park
11 Madison Avenue
New York, NY
10010
212.889.0905

Gabriel Kreuther
41 West 42nd Street
New York, NY
10036
212.257.5826

Established in 1954, Relais & Châteaux is an association of more than 560 landmark hotels and restaurants operated by independent innkeepers, chefs, and owners who share a passion for their businesses and a desire for authenticity in their relationships with their clientele. • Relais & Châteaux is established around the globe, from the Napa Valley vineyards to French Provence to the beaches of the Indian Ocean. It offers an introduction to a lifestyle inspired by local culture and a unique dip into human history. • Relais & Châteaux members have a driving desire to protect and promote the richness and diversity of the world's cuisines and traditions of hospitality.

Gary Danko
800 North Point Street
San Francisco, CA
94109
415.749.2060

Glenmere Mansion
634 Pine Hill Road
Chester, NY
10918
845.469.1900

Homestead Inn – Thomas Henkelmann
420 Field Point Road
Greenwich, CT
06830
203.869.7500

Hotel Les Mars
27 North Street
Healdsburg, CA
95448
707.433.4211

Hotel Wailea
555 Kaukahi Street
Wailea, HI
96753
808.874.0500

Jean-Georges
1 Central Park West
New York, NY
10023
212.299.3900

Lake Placid Lodge
144 Lodge Way
Lake Placid, NY
12946
518.523.2700

L'Auberge Carmel
Monte Verde Street at 7th Avenue
Carmel-by-the-Sea, CA
93921
831.624.8578

Magee Homestead
6429 WY HWY 130
Saratoga, WY
82331
307.327.2031

Manresa Restaurant
320 Village Lane
Los Gatos, CA
95030
408.354.4330

Meadowood Napa Valley
900 Meadowood Lane
St. Helena, CA
94574
707.531.4788

Menton
354 Congress Street
Boston, MA
02210
617.737.0099

Ocean House
1 Bluff Avenue
Watch Hill, RI
02891
844.807.4486

Old Edwards Inn and Spa
445 Main Street
Highlands, NC
28741
866.526.8008

Per Se
10 Columbus Circle
New York, NY
10019
212.823.9335

Planters Inn
112 North Market Street
Charleston, SC
29401
843.722.2345

Quince Restaurant
470 Pacific Avenue
San Francisco, CA
94133
415.775.8500

Rancho Valencia Resort & Spa
5921 Valencia Circle
Rancho Santa Fe, CA
92067
858.756.1123

Royal Blues Hotel
45 Northeast 21st Avenue
Deerfield Beach, FL
33441
954.857.2929

Saison
178 Townsend Street
San Francisco, CA
94107
415.828.7990

Single Thread Farm – Restaurant – Inn
131 North Street
Healdsburg, CA
95448
707.723.4646

The Charlotte Inn
27 South Summer Street
Edgartown, MA
02539
508.627.4151

The Fearrington House
2000 Fearrington Village Center
Pittsboro, NC
27312
919.542.2121

The French Laundry
6640 Washington Street
Yountville, CA
94599
707.944.2380

The Inn at Dos Brisas
10000 Champion Drive
Washington, TX
77880
979.277.7750

The Inn at Hastings Park
2027 Massachusetts Avenue
Lexington, MA
02421
781.301.6660

The Inn at Little Washington
Middle and Main Streets
Washington, VA
22747
540.675.3800

The Inn of the Five Graces
150 East De Vargas Street
Santa Fe, NM
87501
505.992.0957

The Ivy Hotel
205 East Biddle Street
Baltimore, MD
21202
410.514.6500

The Little Nell
675 East Durant Street
Aspen, CO
81611
970.920.4600

The Lodge at Glendorn
1000 Glendorn Drive
Bradford, PA
16701
814.362.6511

The Pitcher Inn
275 Main Street
Warren, VT
05674
802.496.6350

The Point
222 Beaverwood Road
Saranac Lake, NY
12983
518.891.5674

The Ranch at Rock Creek
79 Carriage House Lane
Philipsburg, MT
59858
406.859.6027

The Swag
2300 Swag Road
Waynesville, NC
28785
828.926.0430

The Wauwinet
120 Wauwinet Road
Nantucket, MA
02584
508.228.0145

Triple Creek Ranch
5551 West Fork Road
Darby, MT
59829
406.821.4600

Twin Farms
452 Royalton Turnpike
Barnard, VT
05031
802.234.9999

Weekapaug Inn
25 Spray Rock Road
Westerly, RI
02891
844.211.4493

Winvian Farm
155 Alain White Road
Morris, CT
06763
860.567.9600

PHOTOGRAPHY CREDITS

AUBERGE DU SOLEIL: Bing's Design, pages 138–139; Steph Grant Photography, page 137; Ryan Greenleaf Photography, page 141; Briana Marie Photography, page 135; Nate Puhr Photography, page 140; Trinette Reed, page 136; Alexander Rubin Photography, pages 131, 132–133

AUBERGE SAINT-ANTOINE: Cagdas Yoldas (photographer)/ Foudamour, Mélanie Aubin (designer), pages 49 (top left), 111 (bottom right), 143 (top left), 144–153, 213 (bottom right)

LAS MAÑANITAS: Courtesy of Las Mañanitas, pages 154–167

MAGEE HOMESTEAD: Courtesy of Magee Homestead, pages 169–177

OCEAN HOUSE: Dave Robbins Photography, pages 112–129

OLD EDWARDS INN & SPA: Terry Clark, pages 2–3; Christina Devictor, Someplace Wild, pages 13 (bottom), 33 (top and bottom); Miranda Grey Weddings, page 10; Sarah Ingram Photography, pages 20–21, 22, 23, 26–27, 30, 31, 48 (top), 213 (top right); Paul Johnson Photography, page 13 (top); Courtesy of Old Edwards Inn & Spa, page 8; Genya O'Neall, Vue Photography, pages 25, 49 (top right), 111 (top right); Lydia Phillips, Mintwood Photo Co., page 19; Madeline Trent Photography, pages 29, 48 (bottom); Perry Vaile Photography, pages 14–15, 110 (bottom); The Willetts Wedding Photography, page 17

POST HOTEL & SPA: Cynthia Bendle/Studio 112, pages 229, 230–231; Brittany Esther/Brittany Esther Photography, page 233; Erika and Lanny Mann/Two Mann Studios, pages 224, 234–235; Kirstie Tweed/Orange Girl Photography, 226–227, 232

THE FEARRINGTON HOUSE INN: Krystal Kast Photography, pages 50–75

THE INN AT DOS BRISAS: Koby Brown, pages 34–47, 49 (bottom right); Koby Brown for Martha Stewart Weddings, page 111 (top left)

THE IVY HOTEL: Nessa K Photography, pages 111 (bottom left), 215–223

THE RANCH AT ROCK CREEK: Belathée Photography, page 91 (top); Belathée Photography, Habitat Events, pages 4, 98–99, 143 (bottom left); Rebecca Hollis Photography, Greenwood Events, page 86; Elizabeth Lanier Photography, page 91 (bottom); Elizabeth Lanier Photography, Habitat Events, pages 92, 93, 96, 97; Elizabeth Lanier Photography, Spurlé Gul Studio for Papergoods and Calligraphy, pages 94–95; Christian Oth Photography, Habitat Events, pages 88–89; Nirav Patel Photography, Habitat Events, pages 101, 102–103, 104, 105, 106 (left and right), 107, 108, 109

THE WICKANINNISH INN: Chelsea Gray Photography, pages 179, 182, 183 (left and right), 184; Jeremy Koreski, page 185; Paul Levy, pages 143 (bottom right), 180–181, 186, 187, 213 (bottom left); Kyler Vos, pages 142 (bottom), 143 (top right)

WEEKAPAUG INN: Henry + Mac, pages 76–85, 212 (top and bottom)

WINVIAN FARM: JAGStudios, pages 6, 49 (bottom left), 110 (top), 142 (top), 188–211, 213 (top left), 236

First published in the United States of America in 2021 by
Rizzoli International Publications, Inc.
300 Park Avenue South
New York, NY 10010
www.rizzoliusa.com

Publisher: Charles Miers
Editor: Sandra Gilbert Freidus
Design: Doug Turshen with Steve Turner
Production Manager: Barbara Sadick
Editorial Assistants: Elizabeth Smith,
Hilary Ney, Rachel Selekman
Managing Editor: Lynn Scrabis

Printed in China

2021 2022 2023 2024 / 10 9 8 7 6 5 4 3 2 1

ISBN: 978-0-8478-6945-9

Library of Congress Control Number: 2021937246

Visit us online:
Facebook.com/RizzoliNewYork
instagram.com/rizzolibooks
twitter.com/Rizzoli_Books
pinterest.com/rizzolibooks
youtube.com/user/RizzoliNY
issuu.com/Rizzoli